"You CAN go through the fire and come out not even smelling like smoke!"

Going Through the Fire

Pastor Rhonda Spencer

Other Resources by Rhonda Spencer
Going Through the Fire Workbook
The perfect companion to Going Through the Fire. Dig deep into what God's Word is saying to you when you go through tough times.

Victory Every Day & Victory Every Day Workbook
The devil is already defeated. He's not even a contender! Learn to live in victory every single day, regardless of your circumstances.

No More Hurt & No More Hurt Workbook
Be healed and learn to live in freedom from emotional pain and offense.

God Cannot Lie
Cancer is defeated! Rhonda's testimony, with documented proof of the miracle God did in her body. Follow her walk of faith through the process.

His Daily Word
A 365-day devotional co-authored with her husband, Dr. Micheal Spencer.

Living a WOW Life
A 31-day devotional for women.

All other resources are available at:

www.RhondaJSpencer.com & www.amazon.com.

Going Through the Fire is printed by KDP Direct Publishing (an Amazon company). It is available at amazon.com and other retail outlets.

Going Through the Fire

Foreword

My name is Micheal Spencer and I had the tremendous blessing of being married to Rhonda Jeanne Spencer for almost 32 years. She was not only the love of my life, but the mother of my three children, and Mami of our 6 grandchildren. We married when she was very young, and together, we entered the ministry. From day one, we've known that God loves people and desires to see them snatched from hell and brought to the saving knowledge of our wonderful Jesus.

RHONDA LOVED PEOPLE! There was no question that she loved to love God's family and she served them with all her heart. Together, we established His Tabernacle Family Church in 1998 with just five people. Over the last 24 years, we've loved people to life and grew five seeds to well over a thousand souls with many campuses and pastors. We have been so privileged to speak into their lives. Rhonda Jeanne was an author of multiple books, but her passion was to be an ear, heart, and mouthpiece for pastors' wives. She was passionate to encourage, cry with, celebrate, and push pastors' wives to health, wholeness, and greatness.

On January 29th at 5:04 am after a two-year fight of faith, my adoring wife went home to be with her Lord. Our hearts were broken, not just for ourselves, but for the many lives she impacted daily with her sincere love and compassion.

The powerful portion is that she does not need a tombstone to be remembered. Her legacy of love was not buried, but a new flame was ignited and fueled. Her passionate care for pastors' wives had been taken to another level. We are purchasing a home near a beach and naming it The RHONDAJEANNE

—

4

House for pastors' wives to go and be refreshed. The home will scream of her kindness, ensuring that pastors' wives feel special, loved, energized, and healed. The RHONDAJEANNE House will be a FREE place for them to go to get refreshed and have life spoken into them.

Pastor Rhonda finished her last book entitled, "Going Through The Fire," but never published it. We are publishing this writing and all the proceeds will go to paying for the airplane tickets for the pastors' wives who need to go and grab a week of renewal at The RHONDAJEANNE House at no cost to them.

If you would like to sow into the house and Rhonda's legacy, please use the QR code below to sow a seed.

Rhonda is not dead; but so very much alive in heaven. She is still here on earth and continues to make an impact through her writings of, "No More Hurt," "Victory Every Day," "Going Through The Fire," "His Daily Word Devotional," and other books, which are available on Amazon or on her website, www.empoweringpastorswives.com.

THANK YOU FOR LOVING HER AND ALLOWING HER LIFE AND IMPARTATION TO AFFECT AND INFECT YOUR LIFE. SHE WILL BE WAITING FOR US ALL IN HEAVEN. LIVE LIFE AND HAVE FUN!

Get up, Dress up, Show Up, Never Give Up!
NOT THIS TIME DEVIL – NOT ANY TIME!

Chapter 1
Going Through the Fire!

Going through the fire!

If you're reading this you probably are or have gone through it. Maybe you're saying, "I'm really going through it right now." This book is about how to go through the fire and come out on the other side not even smelling like smoke. Because you can. You can go through it and come out victorious. I'm not just saying this. It is not a cliche. I'm sharing my story. I'm saying this to you from a place of knowing what I'm talking about. Whatever it is that you're facing today, or whatever it is that you will face in your lifetime of going through it, you can make it through victorious. You can make it out the other side, not even smelling like smoke.

Listen, the devil cannot write your story. God already wrote it. He wrote it for whatever you're going through and whatever you're *gonna* go through. You know the end of the story. You get through it. This is not just my story; make this your story. The end of your story can be victory every day.

When you go into that lion's den, guess what? You're coming out unscathed. When you go through the fire, you're coming out not even smelling like smoke. When you go through famine, you're gonna have abundance. When you're in the desert places, you'll be watered. That can be your story too, no matter what it is that you're facing today.

You might be saying "I've got this," right? Have you ever been to that place in your mind? Listen, the truth is without Jesus, *we are nothing*. The Word of the Lord is what's quick and powerful.

As you read through this book, some of the stuff that you've been facing is going to be cut off. It's going to be transferred to victory. Discouragement is going to be turned into encouragement. As you read this, the Word of God is going to change your life!

Isaiah 43:2 (NLT) says, *"When you go through deep waters* [you're going through it, right?] *I will be with you. When you go through rivers of difficulties…"*

My husband and I were watching a cowboy show where they got stuck in white waters with their canoe. That's like rivers of difficulty. Have you been in that place where it's just taken you into that river of difficulty? It's tossing and turning you. It's pulling you under, dropping you off waterfalls, and just rolling you around.

…When you go through rivers of difficulty you will not drown. You will not drown! You will not drown! *When you walk through the fire of oppression you will not be burned up. The flames will not consume you.* That's what God has to say about your victory, about your circumstance, and about what you're going through.

This is where my current story comes in. Four years ago, I was diagnosed with cancer and God miraculously took it away. I have picture-proof evidence. Doctors' reports showed it was gone from my body. Then the devil tried taking me out again a year and a half ago around Thanksgiving time. I was diagnosed with stage 4 cancer and given two weeks to live.

This was that "maybe this time" for me because it was a time when my husband and I had been personally attacked by people that we'd loved and invested in. So the enemy was like, "maybe this time I can get them to be offended and I can take her out." He's been trying to silence my voice from the day that I was born. "Maybe this time" with all the pressures and responsibilities.

"Maybe this time" when the doctor's report didn't include a miracle, (the doctors' reports coming back just kept getting worse and worse).

"Maybe this time I can get her to be too afraid."

"Maybe this time my whispers can convince her that she's gonna die and not live."

"Maybe this time after a year and a half of fighting the good fight of faith I can get her to be too tired that she'll just give up and throw in the towel."

"Maybe this time the pain will be too great and she will turn her back on God." (I had many pain-filled nights.)

"Maybe this time…"

Listen, I'm not just talking about my story; this is your story too. These are the temptations whispered in your ears too.

"Maybe this time?"

Don't ever let the devil win with his "maybe this time" because look, a year and a half ago I was given two weeks to live, and here I am, by the faithfulness of God, still standing! And you would not know, you would not even know, except for I'm telling you now the things that I had been through in the last year and a half.

Let me stop and say this - doctors aren't bad. Doctors are awesome, awesome people but the only thing they have is their science and data. That's literally what my surgeon told me when I told her, "My God is my healer and you're gonna see a miracle. You're gonna see God heal my body. You're gonna see God move in my life." She looked at me and she said, "But I don't have any data on this faith stuff that you're talking about."

Doctor, here's your data. I am your data.

Just a few weeks ago (and I'll get to this part), I had just been through hell and back and was still standing. I thanked my doctor for what she did, and she looked at me (this doctor with no data in the beginning) and said, "There is no medical way; this is all you. Whatever it is you're doing, you need to keep doing it." There's the data that we get to give as Christians.

I want to tell you right now that trouble happens. Look at you, the Church, condemning people that have troubles spring up in their lives. You say, "Ooh, what kind of private sin do they have?" or "What do they have going on?" Shame on us for not rallying behind people and supporting them and holding them up with faith. Trouble happens, but defeat does not have to be the final outcome.

When trouble happens for a Christian, it looks different. It *should* look different than when trouble happens for the world. It's biblical for trouble to happen, but it's not biblical for you to be defeated.

The Word of God talks to us about trouble in John 16:33. It says, i*n this world, you will have trouble.* So stop your condemning and start building up and encouraging! Listen, it's a good thing for that to be the first thing to ask yourself: "Where in my life have I gone astray? What have I done wrong?" That's okay, we can ask those things. But defeat is not your ending. Defeat is not your story. No matter what it is you are facing or why you are facing it, defeat is not your story. It isn't today, it isn't tomorrow, and it never will be. According to John 16:33, trouble is a guarantee.

"See, Rhonda. I told you there is trouble." Trouble is normal, but the verse doesn't end there. That's not the end of the scripture. It's just the intro. It says in this world, you'll have tribulation, trials, distresses, frustrations (amen to that, right?). But it also says, "Be of good cheer, be encouraged, be confident, be certain, be undaunted."

When you face that trouble, be undaunted. Be courageous when you face that thing. "For I have overcome the world. I have deprived it of its power to harm you and I have conquered it for you, no matter what." Even when you can't see it, even when you can't feel it. You can't move from the truth; from the Word of God that says, "I have overcome that thing. I have deprived it of its power to harm you."

I am here today and can tell you *God has deprived cancer of its power to harm me* and to take life from me. God has deprived it of its power and anything that goes along with it. God is greater than cancer.

You may say, "Yeah, yeah." But the reality is, in the trouble, there are moments when the devil's whispering in your ear, "You're gonna die. You're not gonna make it. You're not strong enough for this. You're not chosen like a pastor or an evangelist. You're not good enough for this."

Oh listen, I dare anybody to say that I'm standing here today because I'm a pastor. You weren't there in the middle of the night when I was laying out on the floor in so much pain and agony that I couldn't sleep for days on end. But I chose to believe what God said about me. I chose to stand up in the middle of the fire so that people looking in could see that God was with me in that fire!

Faith comes from our choices; not from who we are or what position we hold. It comes from our choices to fight the good fight of faith and to stand up. This is my motto: Get up, Dress up and Show up. You've got to get up, dress up and show up no matter what it is you're facing. It confounds the enemy. He says, "Wait didn't I put cancer on her? Didn't I tell her she couldn't live past two weeks? What is she doing standing up?"

I preached so many sermons when I could barely stand, but I would get up and I would preach just to defy the devil. I can't stand him and I don't want him to get any glory from my life. I would tell my husband or Carla, who would travel with me, "If I fall over, just stand me back up, cause I'm gonna keep going. I'm not quitting. I'm not stopping." That's what we've got to do with trouble.

When you're going through it, don't give up, don't quit, don't give in to the enemy's lies. He's a liar. If he tells you you're gonna die, you can say, "Well, he's a liar. I know I'm gonna live because all he can say are lies. All he's got are lies." Trouble happens, but it's how you handle your trouble that's different.

As a child of God and as a kingdom person, you get to handle trouble differently. You get to stand in the face of it. You see, for me, *faith is the only option*. Seriously, if we think about it logically and look at it, faith is the only option. When I was lying there on the floor in so much pain, what is the alternative to faith? Just stay in that place? Die? Curl up? Give up? Depression? They tried to give me anxiety pills on a regular basis because "How can you not? It's okay. It's normal. It's normal, you can take these. It's normal for you to feel depressed and discouraged." No, it's not! It is *not* normal to feel that way. That is not my option. Faith is the only option for living. Faith is the only option for abundant life. We have promises. The only thing I'm going to walk in is faith. That's my only option.

When the devil tells you, "Just give up," kick him in the face! What are you, stupid, devil? You think I'm gonna give up? That it's my alternative to faith? It's not an alternative at all. It is a lie that giving up is a better option. Throwing in the towel on your marriage is a better option? "This is too hard. I just can't do it" - that's a better option? No way! Faith is the only option and guess what? When you stand in faith, you get to stand in the joy and the peace of God as you walk through the fire. People will look at your life and every doctor and every nurse is just completely confounded! They're like, "You don't look like what you're going through. You don't look like what you've been through." And every time that happened to me, I was faithful to say, "It is Jesus, it is Jesus, it is Jesus."

When you have Jesus and you walk in faith as your only option, people are gonna be confounded. They're gonna look at you in the middle of that fire and be like, "That is not possible." I've heard it so many times. I have been in the emergency room. I've had life-saving and life-altering emergency surgeries. I've been through chemotherapy (something I said I would never in my life do) and radiation, but through it all, they kept looking at me and saying "You don't look like what you're going through." That's the difference between faith and the alternative to faith. I'm not gonna look like anything the devil tries to put on me because I'm not wearing it. I'm not wearing that coat of oppression, depression, giving up, anxiety, taking meds, curling up and dying. I don't accept "This is just your portion" or "This is just your lot in life." I'm not taking that coat and putting it on. You don't have to either. You don't have to accept the stuff that the devil throws at you.

Every time I was doing chemotherapy, I would have a ball of chemotherapy that I had to wear. I preached with it on. We went on Facebook Live and we taught Rock Solid Faith while I was wearing a ball with chemotherapy pumping through my body. My declaration every time I had to put that thing on was: *"No deadly thing shall harm me (Luke 10:19 KJV - Behold, I give unto you power to tread on serpents and scorpions, and over all the power of the enemy: and nothing shall by any means hurt you.). I can drink poison and it will not harm me (Mark 16:18 KJV - They shall take up serpents; and if they drink any deadly thing, it shall not hurt them; they shall lay hands on the sick, and they shall recover.)."*

I would just declare that it cannot harm me. The effects of radiation cannot harm or damage my body. You know what? It's a loud voice that comes flooding in against you. I'm not pretending that it was easy! Many days it took everything that I had in me to even get up out of bed. But faith is my only option, and when you've done everything that you can do to stand, just "Stand therefore!" So many times I said, "God I just don't even know what to do." I would hear Him say "Then just stand. Just stand therefore."

Stand on the Word of God. *Continuously* stand on the Word of God. I can tell you there is an absolute God with an absolute Word and I have absolute faith in Him. Not because of a theory, but because I've walked through the fire. I've walked through it night and day. There were times I'd be up all night. Many nights, I was up laying on the floor in pain. I mean, I had almost a year of maybe 2 hours of sleep a night. For almost eight months, doctors kept telling me I'm gonna die. It was the science; it wasn't the doctors. Doctors are not evil. Doctors are awesome. The way you get through the fire without being burned and without a "maybe this time" creeping up on you and taking you out is with a deep relationship with an absolute God.

If you want to be able to walk through anything life brings you (and boy do we need to be in that position in today's world), you need to make sure you have a deep relationship with your faithful, awesome, absolute God. Walk with Him and talk with Him. Get in the Word of God. Have a relationship with God. It's not just for pastors. It's for every single one of us. Just talk to God. Come to Him with everything. *Philippians 4:6 NLT says, "Don't worry about anything; instead, pray about everything. Tell God what you need, and thank him for all he has done."*

The Word of God says to bring everything to Him - every business deal, every relationship problem, every concern, and everything that you encounter - just bring it to God.

"Hey God, what do I do with this?"

"Good morning Holy Spirit. How do I handle this today?"

"What do you want me to do today?"

You must have a deep relationship with God that is immovable. It makes *you* immovable. It makes you so that you will stand on solid rock. Matthew 7:24-25 is about sinking sand and solid rock. You stand on the solid rock if you listen to and obey the Word of God.

If we have the alternative of faith, we're building our lives on sinking sand. If we go with the alternative (like the reports of what medical science says is normal) we're building our lives on sinking sand and we should not think that we will stand. There is only collapse on sinking sand. *That* is the alternative. Nobody wants that alternative. Stop signing up for that alternative!

When the devil gives you that alternative, don't buy into it! When people come whispering in your ear, don't follow their words; follow the Word of God. When we follow the Word of God, it says we're building our lives on solid rock. And listen, I love this so much because God doesn't promise that life's gonna be rainbows, lollipops, fluffy clouds, and everything's gonna be perfect. He doesn't promise that. But He does promise you victory and He promises you're gonna go through it.

In this parable (Matthew 7:24-25), Jesus says "when" the rain falls, not "if" it falls. It says *when* the rain falls. Here, let's read it: *"Everyone who hears these words of mine and acts on them will be like a wise man [farsighted not just living in the moment, thinking about the future, practical, sensible] who built his house on the rock and then rain fell…"*

Oh, you know, we can all handle a little bit of rain, can't we? We can handle a little bit, and then the *floods*… so now it's flooding. It's not just raining. The water is overtaking you. It says *when* torrents of waves of floodwater rush over the top of your life and knock you down. You've seen video footage of floods. Maybe you've even been in one. A flood can sweep everything away that's in its path. Maybe it's trying to sweep you away now. Torrents came and the winds blew. It's all hell breaking loose right now. Rain, floodwaters, torrents, and then the winds blew and slammed against the house. Have any of you ever felt like that? The floodwaters, the torrents, torrents, torrents, torrents, torrents, torrents? The wind is now slamming on my house.

It's in those moments when the devil's like, "Maybe this time I can get them to quit." He gets so excited about that. Come on, Christian, rise up! When those things come against you; when those torrents come; when the floodwaters come; when the wind is slamming on you; you can stand and *stand therefore* knowing that you are on solid rock. The end of that says that you cannot fall because you have been founded on the rock.

I can't die. The devil can't kill me because I've been founded on the rock. The Word of God says you shall live and not die. It says that He will heal me, that He is my healer, that He is my restorer. So no matter what it looks like, no matter if the floodwaters have completely overtaken me and the wind is now slamming me with those reports, I cannot fall.

You cannot fall when you build yourself on the rock, and when you stand on what the
Word of God says instead of what the world says. You will not fall. You'll go through anything and everything in victory every day.

The devil's so dumb. He's so dumb! But you know what? How many times does he win? I've seen it. I've seen some of the best taken out by "maybe this time." I don't know about you, but I hate losing! I hate when the devil wins even more. I will never give the devil a win in my life. Never! I'm too stubborn for it. I hate him that much. I hate what he does that much. I'm not giving it to him in my life, and I pray that you will never give it to him in your life.

Faith is the only option. Keep standing. Keep standing even if you have to tie your Bible to you. If you have to strap the Word of God onto you, then you do whatever you've got to do. But you just keep standing! It's the only way. The alternative is not an option. It's not one you want to have to live with. Come on! Some of you need to rise up out of that place right now! Some of you are in the middle of it. The floodwaters have overtaken you, the torrents are coming, and the wind is slamming on you. I need you to stand right up in that place! Come on, right now, I want you to stand right up out of that place. Stand up out of that place! Stand up out of that place! Stand up out of that place! (I hope you physically stood up. If not, do it now.)

The devil's not sending rescue boats to you. You've gotta do it. You've gotta stand up out of that place! Oh, it's breaking off of you right now! It's breaking off of you because it says when you act on the Word of God, you're standing on solid rock. Sinking sand has to disappear. I am so excited about God. In the middle of my trouble, in my hardest hours, that's what I do! I stand right up out of that place. I get up, I dress up, and I show up because the devil's not getting a win in my life.

"Stand therefore." It's found in Ephesians 6:13-14. *"Therefore take up the whole armor of God, that you may be able to withstand in the evil day, having done all, to stand. Stand therefore…"* It's so simple. We make it so complicated like, "I don't know what to do." "I don't know what decision to make." "I don't know what choice to make." It's not that complicated. All you've got to do is *stand therefore*. Stand on the Word of God.

Romans 8:28 has been my scripture. It says, *"All things work together for good."* All things work together for good for those who love Him. Again, it's not automatic. Not everything is going to work together for good. It says it works together for good *for those who love Him*. I know, I know, I know, everybody loves God. No, let God define what that means. God says in John 14:15, *"If you love Me, you keep My Word."* When you keep His Word, I'm here to tell you that all things work together for your good.

Now I'm going to get really real with you. After a year and a half of living hell all around us, but walking in the Kingdom and celebrating every day, the fact that I have breath in my lungs and I'm still here…I mean there are some days when just waking up overwhelms me. I get to still be here. But I'm going to get so real with you because I think you need to hear it.

Too many people get to this place and you feel like you're the only one. The devil's going to tell you you're the only one that feels like this and that you should give up. During Christmas, they had stopped telling me I was going to die and I was in a much more confident place. I ended up back in the hospital, again fighting for my life. During surgery, they came to a place where the doctor called my husband and said that she didn't think that she could go through with it. I was bleeding so badly that they didn't think they would be able to finish the operation. They ended up giving me six transfusions – nine units of blood, four units of plasma, and platelets. So they pretty much replaced my whole blood system. And much like Jesus in the wilderness, it was another "maybe this time" that the enemy had thrown at me. I mean, I had conquered all of it. I was still standing. And there I found myself. I didn't even know. I was sedated and I had no idea what was going on. I ended up being in the hospital for 12 days. I wasn't even home for Christmas. I got to a place where I was physically done. I had nothing left in me. I hadn't eaten in almost three weeks. I was so physically frail that I could not fight. You know my motto, Get up, Dress up, Show up? I physically couldn't do it.

So I know. I know what it feels like. I'm here to tell you, I don't judge. I know what it feels like. I had no physical strength left to fight the good fight of faith. It was just gone.

That's a scary place when you've been able to – with great willpower and strength – be that strong person. I had always been able to muster it up inside of me. But to be at a place where I could no longer do that, I had nothing. My physical body couldn't fight for me any longer. I was alone.

At the time, you couldn't have anybody with you due to the pandemic. So through all of this, throughout the year, I was alone in hospitals on a regular basis. I was alone in this hospital at my weakest physical and emotional moment. I had nothing. I didn't care to respond to my phone anymore. I didn't have anything left in me. The greatest part about being a child of God is that we are three-part beings. I've never experienced it like I experienced it this past year. I actually got to feel all three parts of my being. My flesh, we already know it was done. Then my soul, which is the mind, emotions, will, and intellect: I was so heavily drugged, and many of you know what I'm talking about. When you're on heavy medications, it alters your will, your thoughts, and your emotions. So now I couldn't even fight with my mind because I was so drugged and so medicated. I'm a strong person but I didn't have the willpower anymore because of the drugs taking over my life. In that moment, I actually just wished they would drug me to death and I'd just be gone and done with it all.

So I get being at the place where you just want to quit and have nothing left to fight with. But there was something that happened in that hospital room, and I want you to know I'm not the only three-part being. Every single one of us is created in the image of God, with a body, a soul, (mind, emotions, and will), and a spirit. In that moment when I was lying there for 12 days, at the end, I was just not caring anymore; just done. My spirit man was still there, still present.

I want you to know that when you're squeezed, you're gonna find out what's been put inside of you. So you're going to want to make sure of what's inside of you before you get in a position of being squeezed. Everything that I had put inside of me, - even with all of that inside of me, *even with all of that* - I still was at that place where I couldn't fight. But I had a *spirit* man! I'm so thankful! I am so thankful that it is not up to me and my own ability.

So I put on some praise music by my head. Not that I wanted to. I hadn't up until that point. I complained. I cried. I whined. But I put the praise music up by my head, and my spirit man started to grow inside of me – and grow, and grow, and grow, *and grow*. When I couldn't do it, when I had nothing, my spirit man stood up inside of me and it began to fight for me. It rose me up out of that bed. I didn't have to do it in my own strength.

God will fight for you! Romans 8:11 says *"But if the Spirit of Him who raised Jesus from the dead dwells in you, He who raised Christ from the dead will also give life to your mortal bodies through His Spirit who dwells in you."* So it doesn't matter if you don't have any strength. It doesn't matter if you don't have the willpower left. It doesn't matter if you're at the end of it all. It's good because in your weakness, He is made strong, and your weaknesses show that He is the only way.

If you have Jesus in your life, then whatever it is you're facing right now, whatever it is you've given up on (It might not be sickness. It might be fear. It might be a relationship. It might be your job. It might be financial.), you have Christ, and the same spirit that raised Him from the dead dwells inside of you. I don't know what it is that you've given up on, but I'm telling you, I'm living proof that it will actually quicken your physical body to a place that it will raise you right up out of that deathbed. It'll raise you right up out of depression. It will raise you right up out of quitting. It'll raise you right up out of fear. That same spirit that raised Christ from the dead *dwells inside of you!* Maybe it took everything you had in you to even read this book today. Maybe it takes everything inside of you to get up in the morning. That's okay because you have a spirit man that'll raise up and fight for you!

1 John 4:4 says, *"Greater is He that is in me than he that is in the world."* Greater is He that is in me than he that is in the world. Greater is he that is in *YOU* than he that is in the world. Don't quit. Don't give up. Don't let the devil win in your life. He's a liar, he's a loser, and he's already defeated. He just wants you to join the defeated team. How many want to join the defeated team? No, that's just dumb. Here we have the undefeated team: Our God, our absolute. And then we have the already defeated team over there. Who are you signing up with? We're signing up with the undefeated team! But that's a choice. It's a daily choice. It's a moment-by-moment choice. It doesn't just happen. Make sure you're signing up with the undefeated team. Bring everything that comes at you before God. Let that spirit that's inside of you rise up and fight for you because God has promised. What He has for you is exactly what Jesus says in John 10:10 – *abundant life.*

Come on, Christian! Trouble's gonna happen. I am tired of the church being defeated! Trouble's gonna happen! Stop counting yourself out because some trouble happened in your life. Trouble happens to us all. The rain falls on the just and the unjust alike. Rise up, Christian! We're to do it differently. We're to walk through unscathed. We're to walk through unburned. We're to walk through and still be standing at the end of it. I don't care what happens around me or outside of me. I am more confident than ever that if anything's thrown at me, here I am! I'll still be standing when the dust settles, I promise you! My husband and I are gonna still be standing here! Our church will still be standing here! You will still be standing! Come on! You will still be standing! Kick the devil in the teeth with me! I love victory! I love victory way too much to sign up for that defeated team! I refuse to sign up for anything he has to say, any report he has to give, or anything science has to say.

Listen, we're not natural. We are supernatural. *We are supernatural.* It's about time we walk in the supernatural. Walk in the supernatural in your finances. Walk in the supernatural! Let's just do that really quickly and look at the area of finances.

So, we can just do our little offering portion and you can give as you leave. No, walk supernaturally in your finances! Remember, He says, *"If you love me, keep my commandments"* and *that's* when all things are going to work together for good. So His Word tells us to tithe, to *"bring all the tithe"* (Malachi 3:10). The word tithe simply means ten percent. It's not something pastors made up. *"Bring all the tithe into the storehouse and I'll open the windows of heaven and pour out a blessing…"* Listen, He will give you bread in a famine. He'll give you seed to sow. He'll bless you. He takes pleasure in the prosperity of his children (Psalm 35:27). It's time that Christians start walking in victory in their finances and in their businesses. Walk in victory! Don't give up. Don't throw in the towel. When you've done everything to stand, you just keep standing on the Word of God and the Word of God will fight for you. It'll make a way where there is no way. You'll outshine everybody else in the middle of a pandemic, in the middle of a recession, and in the middle of a famine.

Guess what? The children of God are blessed! We're blessed when we go, blessed when we come, blessed in our storehouse, and blessed in our basket. That's the children of God (Deuteronomy 28:5-8). We need to start walking in it! We need to walk in victory no matter what the trouble is, no matter what the enemy brings. Don't let it be "maybe this time." "Maybe this time I'll get them just so mad at that person." "Ooh, maybe this time I'll just get them to be a part of that gossip mill." You know those "juicy morsels" (that's what the Word of God calls them in Proverbs 18:8) that lead to death. "Maybe this time." Don't let the devil win! Don't let him get your ear. Don't let him get you because you have a spirit inside of you that he can't touch! He can't touch the spirit inside of you! He can't affect it! He can't dampen it! Whatever you sow to, you'll reap from. So if you're sowing to your spirit man, you are going to reap. There's going to come a time in whatever fashion or form it is that you need to reap from the spirit man; that you need to reap from the supernatural rather than the natural. So, no matter what, even if the doctors have only given you two weeks to live, I'm here to tell you, that you will live and not die! You will live and not die! All you need to do is keep standing!

Keep standing and when all hell breaks loose from every direction; when people lie about you, when people abandon you, when people walk out on you, when your health report is a negative report, and it just keeps coming back negative, when your relationships are broken, when your money's gone, whatever it is, you're coming out victorious! Come on! This is the best year to be alive! It is so exciting because what's happening in the natural is not your story. God gets to write your story and that's prosperity no matter what's happening in the natural! All people are going to be looking at your finances like you're in a fiery furnace and be like, "How? That must be God in there with them."

I would love to lay hands on you, but impartation has come today through the written Word. The scripture has gone forth inside of you and my spirit has spoken to your spirit man. Your spirit man inside of you has been quickening you; quickening your mortal body. Whatever sickness, whatever disease, whatever thing has tried to come upon you, your spirit man has been quickened inside of you and God is raising you up. Your spirit man is standing up and free! Be free of sickness. Be free of disease. Be free of lack. Be free of poverty. Be free of brokenness. Be free of anxiety. Be free of depression. Listen there are things that the scalpel can't touch, *but God*. Going through it just looks different on a Christian.

We've had some stuff broken off of us. You're walking out of today different than you came in! The power of Satan has lost its hold! It's lost its hold on you. Fear has lost its hold. Sickness and disease have lost their hold. Brokenness has lost its hold. Depression has lost its hold. Anxiety has lost its hold. Your spirit man has quickened your physical body. Your physical body has been regenerated under the Word of God. He will cause you to run. This is absolute truth and if you believe it, you go through that fire standing tall and they'll say, "Is that Jesus in there with them? Is that Jesus in there?" Oh, yeah it is! That's my God! That's my God. My surgeon gets to see my God. That oncologist gets to see my God. Those nurses get to see my God. Are you ready to rise up today out of that place? Rise up out of the ashes! Rise up out of the defeat! Rise up out of the addiction! Rise up out of the bondage! Rise up out of the fear!

I'm all about action, so I'm going to have you physically stand to your feet. Stand up in the middle of that thing that's weighing you down. Stand up! Stand up when the torrents are overtaking you! Stand up even though the wind is slamming against you. Stand up! *Stand up!* STAND UP! You're getting up and going through this fire and coming out not even smelling like smoke.

Chapter 2
Maybe This Time

Why is it then, that the devil even comes at us if he knows it's only going to work out for our good? And if he knows every weapon formed can't prosper against us, why does he even try?

The Spirit of God led me to the passage of Jesus' temptation in the wilderness in Luke 4:13. It says that the devil now had ended every temptation and he departed from Him. But you know what? It doesn't end there. That's not where the scripture ends. And so many times we stop right there. You know, it says resist the devil and he will flee. But he's still the devil. He's still our enemy, our adversary, just waiting to pounce on us. Listen to what it says right after that. It says he departed from Him *until a more opportune time*!

"And when the devil had ended every temptation, he temporarily left him." This means he stood off from Him just far enough until another more opportune and favorable time. He has to flee from the Word of God, so he stood right on that line. You know, the line you draw? He stood right on that line with his toes touching it, just waiting for another opportune time. And that's what the Lord spoke to me about victory.

When we win a victory, the devil goes off just far enough to wait for another opportune time. And he says, "Maybe this time. Maybe this time I can get them if it's a more opportune time." So we've got to guard ourselves. 1 Corinthians 10:13 says (and you *need* to get this into your spirit), *"No temptation has overtaken you except what is common to man. But God is faithful, who will not allow you to be tempted beyond what you are able. But with the temptation will also make the way of escape that you may be able to bear it."* So just know that.

Remember that in your battle and victory, and then be alert!

The scripture in 1 Peter 5:8-9 tells us to stay alert and the reason to stay alert. It's this picture of Jesus being tempted in the wilderness. When it was over, the devil finally went and put his toe right on that line, as close as he could get, but far enough away that he had to flee, waiting for an opportune time. So it says to stay alert, watch out for your great enemy, the devil. He prowls around like a roaring lion looking for someone to devour. Stand firm against him and be strong in your faith. Remember that your family of believers all over the world is going through the same kind of suffering that you are. So we must pay attention when we win a victory. That's awesome, but yesterday's victory is not the conclusion of today's unless you apply the same principles. The devil's hoping – like Jesus in the wilderness – that maybe this time he's going to find you too hungry, too famished, too broken, too offended, too tired, or with too much fear coming upon you. I love that He gives this example of temptation, showing that even at your weakest, even when you're all alone, even when you're famished in a desert place, you can have victory over the temptations of the devil, and over everything the enemy brings at us. So we need to remember from the last victory, for our next victory, that we have to apply the same faith.

But the enemy is hoping. He's hoping that maybe this time he's got you isolated out there in the wilderness all by yourself. Maybe this time you got too busy and stopped reading your Word.

"Maybe this time I'll get them because… maybe this time…I'm just waiting for a more opportune time." So just because you won great victories doesn't mean you can put the Word down. The faith shield that won that last victory is the same shield you have for this victory that you're facing. No matter what it is, no matter how tired you are, no matter how discouraged, no matter how long, no matter how many lies the enemy is whispering in your ear, if you hold up the same shield of faith that is still available to you in this next battle, you'll still win a victory.

But he's hoping that you're going to think, "Oh, I just can't. It's been too much. Too much has gone on. I'm just too tired. This has just gone on too long and everybody's abandoned me and left me. I'm not strong enough."

Listen, you made it through that last victory. The same authority is yours today. The enemy is just waiting for you to be too tired. He's just waiting for a more opportune time. In those moments, we have to remember what we already know to be true. You have to remind yourself you still have that shield of faith that will quench every fiery dart. Your shield of faith will quench today's fiery dart. It quenched yesterday's fiery dart and it's going to quench today's fiery dart.

But we get too comfortable in great victories. We're like, "Wow, I'm so super strong." So maybe we start neglecting the Word of God. We're like, "Oh, I got this," and we aren't spending the same amount of time with God that we were while we were in the heat of the battle. Man, the devil is just waiting for you to do that. Maybe life got busy, maybe things shifted and changed. The devil is just waiting for that more opportune time to come in. And listen, you don't have to be afraid that the devil is standing there waiting for the next opportune time at all.

Jesus was betrayed by one of his closest friends. The enemy tried again. He was waiting for that more opportune time. And then, after this betrayal "Oh, surely this is going to be a real opportune time. I'll get you in the Garden of Gethsemane and just overwhelm you with the thought of the suffering that you're going to go through. Maybe this time I'll be able to get you to crumble and be weak enough." But Jesus withstood every single level of temptation, even to the place of going to the cross and dying for us. The devil waited just far enough off till he could have a more opportune time with Jesus. Just think, the enemy of our soul has his henchmen demons standing just far enough off, waiting; especially if it's one that he's got you with in the past.

He's going to stay just as long as you resist. He has to flee. If you resist, even in this moment, he has to flee again. Keep pushing him back to that line. He's not going to leave that line. He's going to stay there. And that's the misconception of victory, we think because we've gotten that victory that he's gone, that the devil is just gone. No, he's not. He's standing on that line where he has to go and he's just waiting, waiting like a roaring lion seeking whom he may devour.

We've got to keep ourselves from being in a vulnerable position. It says stay alert and be aware. We have got to get the Word of God in us so strong and so mighty that it doesn't matter if we've been in the wilderness. We haven't eaten in forty days. We feel abandoned, isolated, alone, broken, and really destitute. It doesn't matter if we put this Word in us and we resist. The devil has to flee every single time. Don't let this be where you are. "Maybe this time, maybe this time I could just overwhelm them." It's crazy to me how you can win such amazing victories and then be faced with something and have any kind of doubt and fear. But how many of you are human? That happens. That's a reality, and that's the misconception that I want to warn you about today – thinking that just because you had that great victory, the devil is just gone, and then you're actually shocked when he comes in and attacks with different things that happen. I mean, listen, he is coordinating things to happen to try to get you discouraged, to try to take you out, to try to create a scenario for a more opportune time.

We cannot be ignorant of the devil's devices. He is waiting in the lurches for a more opportune time. We have got to be aware of that and we've got to be ready. We've got to be reminded that the same power that raised Christ from the dead that brought us to our victory last time, is the very same power that is in you right now. Right now, if you're in one of those more opportune times where things have happened, things have shifted and changed, maybe there was a termination of a job or a shift in location. Maybe it was a struggle, maybe it was some kind of strife, maybe it was some kind of betrayal, maybe it was some kind of offense. Maybe you're in a more opportune time. I want you to hear me. The same spirit that raised Christ from the dead still dwells inside of you and will quicken your mortal body. 1 John 4:4 says, *"Greater is He that is in you than he that is in the world."*

The devil would love for you to believe his lies, his promises are full of deception. We have got to pay his lies no attention. He'll tell you it's just easier to give up. It's just easier to throw in the towel. It's just easier. Oh, listen, it is not easier. He wants you to believe that lie in this more opportune time for him. But we've got to be reminded that we still have a shield of faith that will quench every fiery dart. We still have the Sword of the Spirit that will cut through everything that he brings at us. We still have the authority of Luke 10:19 that we've been authorized against every device of the enemy, no matter what way it comes in. We have got to remain aware and alert, even in our great victories. Yes. Celebrate your victory. But even after your victory, keep feeding your spirit man the Word of God. Stay strong in your spirit. Stay strong in your faith. Don't give the devil a foothold for even a moment. If we give him a foothold, he doesn't just take an inch; he takes a mile. And we have got to be vigilant. Stay alert. According to 1 Peter, we have got to pay attention because he's just hoping. He is just hoping, he is never going to stop trying. And that's what you need to know about victory. Just because you've won a great victory does not mean the devil's going to go away. The Word tells us to be aware of his devices, to stay alert, and to be vigilant. We must pay attention to the lies, the fear, the doubt, and the discouragement that he tries to bring in. We have got to remain aware that for this next victory, it's going to take today's faith and today's fighting. Holding up today's Word in our lives. A lot of times we try to go back to yesterday's victory and think "I shouldn't be dealing with this because look what I've already conquered. Look what I've already defeated. I shouldn't be dealing with that." Listen, the devil is going to continue to try, but he is powerless. He is powerless unless you give up. Do not give up and do not give in no matter what!

Do not let this be a more opportune time and be aware and know he's just waiting for you to isolate. He's waiting for you to get too busy. He's waiting for you to receive that lie that says, *oh, you should just take a break, you should just separate yourself.* All he wants you to believe is his promise that's laced with deception.

Everything the devil says is full of deception. What he's trying to do is get you alone and get you isolated so that he can attack you. But just as Jesus was all alone in the wilderness, He was at the weakest human place that you could be in. And listen, He was all human. In that moment, He was literally feeling just like you would feel if you were all alone in the wilderness. If you hadn't eaten in 40 days, if you had been walking and wandering around in a wilderness place, a dry land with no encouragement, no people to cheer you up. That's where he wants to get you. He wants to get you isolated. But Jesus showed us this example so we could be aware of that. You're never in a place that is more opportune. As long as you remember who you are, as long as you remember your shield, your sword, your authority, your power, your dominion, he gives us surpassing victory, overwhelming victory, even at your worst and weakest moments. Do not let the lie of the enemy tell you that you are too weak or that this is too much, that you just can't go on, that it's just been one thing after another, or that you should just quit. You should just give up. That's what he says to us. He's waiting. He is just waiting for us to bite on that. Just to take it for just a moment.

And man, once you take that, just receiving it even a little bit, he's just going to flood you with every negative emotion and thought in your mind and you're gonna be on a freight train that he will try to destroy you with. But you are never, ever, *ever* in a place where you are too weak. Even if your body is completely famished, if you are completely isolated, or if you've been betrayed. He wasn't just betrayed by Judas. He was also betrayed by Peter; one of his closest disciples, somebody that He loved desperately. Maybe you're in that position. Jesus' victories showed us that even in those moments, you can stand victorious. You can rise above.

Do not allow this to be the enemy's "maybe this time." Maybe this time they will just be too broken." Maybe this time the hit will just be too strong." Maybe it's in your finances. Maybe something has happened. Maybe the devourer has tried to come. Listen! As long as you're a tither and you're obedient to the Word of God in your finances, the Word of God says He will rebuke the devour. I've seen where the devourer has come in and tried to decimate and it could really overwhelm you in a natural sense. But when you know the Word of God, God shows up supernaturally! I've watched it happen!

He sent a raven to feed one of his prophets! He will do whatever He has to do to bring you to victory if we don't quit and if we don't give up in those more opportune times.

So I want you to remain alert. Stay aware that the devil isn't gone just because he fled. When we resist, he has to flee, but he goes just as far as he has to go, and no further. He waits, just pausing there for a more opportune time. Do not allow him to win in your life in those moments when you feel weak. Do not allow him to win. Do not give up on your faith. Do not quit. Apply the exact same faith that you did in every other battle, and that same faith will bring you through this battle, the next battle, and every other battle. You can walk in victory every day. But it's not based on yesterday's victory. You walk in victory every day because you choose faith instead of fear. Faith instead of doubt. You choose to hold your shield up. You choose to resist. We have to resist. It doesn't take a lot; all we have to do is resist. Use the Word of God. Be in the Word. That's what I love to do. Whenever I'm facing anything, I will do a word search in the Bible. I will do a Google word search and say scripture after it. So if it's financial, I just search "finance scriptures." If it's fear, I search "fear scriptures." If it's anger, I search "anger scriptures" etc. And I read everything from the Word of God, filling myself up, putting on my armor, taking my sword out, and holding my shield up.

When we do that, we will overcome. Do not allow the enemy to take over in your thought life in those weak moments. Just fill up. Fuel up the Word, the Word, the Word. The Word is what will get you through every opportune moment that the enemy thinks he has. I can't stand him beating out Christians by just waiting for us to get weak. Waiting for an offense to happen. Waiting for a shift or change in the environment or the atmosphere or the economy or the government. Waiting for something to discourage us. Waiting for a betrayal. He's just waiting for those moments to happen so he can pounce because that's what he does. He plays dirty. He waits till you're weak. And then he tries to get in. That's how he ravages God's people. And I'm so tired of watching people that have had amazing victories be taken out in the next breath because the devil waits. He just waits. We have got to be alert. So today I'm sounding the alarm on this misconception of victory: "Just because I won a victory, I can sit back and relax and I don't have to worry about the devil anymore. I've resisted him. He's all gone."

No, he's not. He's just waiting. He's just waiting for a more opportune time. Maybe this time. And that's not scary. That just means we have to pay attention and be alert. That's all we have to be is alert.

We have to be vigilant. That means constantly and continually paying attention. And it's super easy if we continually get in the Word every single day when we resist. We resist with the Word of God. So, if we are full of the Word of God, it's automatic resisting. It's not even like a struggle. When Jesus was tempted, the Word of God automatically came out of his mouth. And when we are filled with this, if our body is completely weak, if we are in a desert place, if we are all alone, if we are filled with this, what will come out of us? When the devil comes in to tempt, the Word of God is going to come out of you automatically! It's not going to be hard. It's not going to be something that you have to say "Oh, man, I've been fighting this good fight." But now it's going to just come out of you. And that is the exciting part about being alert and being vigilant, it will automatically start coming out of you. When the devil comes in with, "Maybe this time," you'll say, "Oh, man, you are so dumb. Devil, you are so dumb this time. And every time it works out for my good."

This time and every time I want you to tell him that when he comes in like a flood with his lies in your head. I want you to just tell him out loud - *This time and every time it works out for my good.* And you know what? That means better! Not the same. It doesn't work out for *your same*; it works out for your *good*. So I'm just going to get better and better, devil. And when he comes in, you just tell him this time and every time, "No weapon formed against me can prosper this time. And every time, if I resist you, you have to flee. Get out in the name of Jesus." We have authority no matter what. But we've got to be vigilant.

We've got to not get comfortable. Never get comfortable. Your enemy is lurking, is waiting, as a roaring lion seeking whom he may devour. And that's serious business. It's not something we can play around with.

We have got to be solid in the Word, the Word, the Word, the Word. And then it will just come easy and it will come naturally. You will fight the devil just as Jesus fought him in His weakest human moments of life. He fought the enemy simply with the spoken Word. He spoke the Word of the Lord *out loud*, and he caused the devil to have to flee back over that line. I want to keep the devil over that line at all times. Oh man, I get so ticked off when I see him cross over. "You don't even have any right. You're trespassing. Who do you think you are? Get back over that line. You might be able to stand there and watch and wait for a moment. But you don't you dare cross that line. I am never going to let my guard down enough for you to cross that line. Get back. Move over that line and stay out." We have got to be that alert about the enemy and our victories. I have talked to so many people that have had really great victories and they come to me saying, "I don't understand why I'm still having this battle."

As long as you are in this life, the enemy is going to try to come in and tempt you. He's going to try to take you out. You have a choice, though, every new day, how you're going to fight back. You can fight with peace in your spirit. Simply just getting so much of the Word in you that it's what automatically comes out of you. It's not even like it's an effort battle. It's not even like it's a struggling battle. Just keep putting the Word in. And if you have to put it out a whole lot, make sure you put it in a whole lot more. That's the only thing we have to do is remain filled with Jesus. If we get lax and quit putting the Word in, this is what the Bible says the enemy does: Matthew 12:43-45 (NLT) *"When an evil spirit leaves a person, it goes into the desert, seeking rest but finding none. Then it says, 'I will return to the person I came from.' So it returns and finds its former home empty, swept, and in order. Then the spirit finds seven other spirits more evil than itself, and they all enter the person and live there. And so that person is worse off than before. That will be the experience of this evil generation."* This is the "maybe this time" the enemy is hoping for. Stay alert and full of the Word of God.

We have to remind our spirits, remind our souls, and remind our thoughts of what the Word of God has to say - *"Greater is he that is in you than he that is in the world."* This time, next time, and every time, it's the same. Jesus Christ is the same yesterday, today, and forever. So I don't know what position you're in. You may be at a complete place of discouragement or the devil's just dug his lies in there. Jesus is the same yesterday, today, and forever. He's still greater. He still has overcome that for you. He still has surpassing victory. He has planned a way out. You will be victorious. Do not give in. Do not give up. Simply pick up the Word of God and fill yourself.

The only thing I want to come out of me when the enemy

comes in and tries to take me out is the Word of God. I don't want there to be an ounce of fear and doubt. And when you put the Word in, you're full of the Word, and there's no room for fear and doubt. There's actually no room for falling and failure. There's no room when you have the Word of God in you.

So be vigilant today. Stay alert and don't rest on yesterday's victory. Don't rest on that. Rest on knowing that the Word of God in you is powerful. It is as powerful today as it was for yesterday's victory. And it'll be as powerful tomorrow as it was for today's victory. It will never, *ever* lose its power.

Chapter 3
God IS With You

God IS with you.

Let's start with Isaiah 43:2. It says *"When you pass through the waters, I will be with you; And through the rivers, they shall not overflow you. When you walk through the fire, you shall not be burned, Nor shall the flame scorch you."*

I want to remind you that God is with you. You are not alone. You have the King of the Universe, the All-Powerful, the Almighty, awesome God. The miracle-working, supernatural God is with you in that very real scenario, circumstance, situation, and anything that is going on around you. I think it's so easy to forget that God is with us. It sounds so cliche and so simple. We should know that, but I promise we forget it. We forget and we get worked up about things and we get to feeling like we're on our own, and like we're the only ones, and that it's a struggle. We get anxious over things because we literally forget. So I just want these scriptures to remind you of Who is on your side, Who is with you, and Who is working inside of you and through you. It's not you. You don't have to do this on your own, no matter what it is. If you're a child of the King, He literally resides inside of you. He goes everywhere with you. You are not alone in this thing, in this venture, in this circumstance, in this situation; you are not alone. God is with you!

I just love the power of the Word because the Word is God, and it is so anointed. I'm praying that the anointing of the Word just surrounds you today and whatever it is that you're going through, you are reminded that God is with you.

Deuteronomy 31:8 says it is the Lord who goes before you. Oh, could we just stop right there? That thing that you've been frustrated about, that you've been afraid of, or nervous or anxious about, stop right now! The Lord goes before you! Isn't that so awesome? I'm reminding us (myself included) that the Lord has already gone before you. How awesome and exciting?! He goes before you. *"He will be with you. He will not leave you or forsake you; do not fear and do not be dismayed."* Oh, I just love the Word of God. When I was reading this, I got so emotional and the anointing just fell on my devotion time. As I was reading the Word of God and how He's with us, how He goes before us, and He won't leave us; like He's NOT. You don't even have to worry that you're going to jump out in faith and He's going to leave you there, or He's going to leave you hanging, or He's going to leave you dangling, or He's going to abandon you. Absolutely not! That scripture just said, *"He goes before you, He's with you, and He will not leave you nor forsake you."* So all through this whole thing, God is with you.

Hebrews 13:5 says *"I will never leave you nor forsake you. I will never, not for a moment."* He's not resting. He's not sleeping. He's not off busy with somebody else. He will never leave you. God is omnipresent. He's able to be with all of us, all the time, every time, everywhere, and in every season, no matter what it is. All the way through, He is with you. Deuteronomy 31:6 says to be strong and courageous. You don't have to be afraid or intimidated. Go ahead and jump out in faith! Be strong and courageous. Do not fear or dread anything, for it is the Lord, your God who goes with you, He will not leave you or forsake you. He's saying it over, and over, and over again so that we know that He is with us. Joshua 1:9 says *"Have I not commanded you? Be strong and courageous. Do not be frightened, and do not be dismayed, for the LORD your God is with you wherever you go."* In the valley, in the fire, in the water, in the darkness, He is with you wherever it is you have to go.

We had a group of people that were being a blessing to somebody in their group and they went to go clean out a house. Well, it was a very, very demonically possessed and oppressed house. I mean, there were pictures in the windows of demons and it was just riddled with demons. It was a horrible, horrible place. The director asked, "Do we go in? What do I do?" and I said, "Yeah! You absolutely go in there because the second you step foot in there, God goes in there with you. Demons have to flee from the anointing. By going in, you're doing more than just cleaning that place up physically. You're spiritually and supernaturally going in and cleaning up that place! Don't be afraid, don't be discouraged. God goes with you wherever you go! It can be completely riddled with the demonic. You could have everything stacked against you, but it doesn't even matter! God goes with you so you can be courageous in that thing that's been intimidating you and that thing that's caused resistance. You just be courageous. Be bold. Be strong. He tells us to because He promises over and over that He's with us and He's not going to leave us or forsake us. Isaiah 41:10 says, *"Fear not, for I am with you…"* Again He's telling us that He'll always be with us.

It's so easy to get caught up and think, "Well, this is just trivial. God doesn't really care about what I'm going through." Yes, He does! It said *every*where you go, in *every*thing, He's with you! So trust that no matter what, you don't have to be afraid. "Fear not for I am with you. Do not be dismayed for I am your God. I will strengthen you. I will help you. I will uphold you." Don't worry, He's got you. He's got His grip on you. You're not gonna fall and collapse and crumble. It says, *"I will uphold you with my righteous right hand, behold all who are incensed against you shall be put to shame and confounded. Those who strive against you shall be as nothing and shall perish. you shall seek those who contend with you but you shall not find them. Those who war against you shall be as nothing at all."* (Isaiah 41:10-12) As nothing at all, that's how we need to see it. It's nothing at all. Compared to the power and presence of God, greater is He that is in me than he that is in the world. *"For I the Lord your God hold your right hand. It is I who say to you 'fear not.' I am the one who helps you."* I love that He's holding your hand through it all.

When people deliver babies, someone comes in and holds their hands. It's awesome to know that in every scenario that we go through, God is right here and His Word is telling us He's holding our hands. You're not alone and, no matter what it is; if it's a test, if it's just some kind of day-to-day thing that comes up, He's holding your hand. He's got you. He's holding you up and He's holding your hand. I mean, you're in a good position. Joshua 1:5 says *"No man shall be able to stand before you all the days of your life. Just as I was with Moses, so shall I be with you. I will not leave you nor forsake you."* And then again in Hebrews 13: 6, it says, *"The Lord is my helper; I will not fear; what can man do to me?"* And just before that, in verse 5, it says *"…I will never leave you nor forsake you."* Matthew 28:20 says, *"I am with you always until the end of the age."*

There is no point in our lives, as children of God, that He is not with us, that He's abandoned you, or left you, or set you aside, or is too busy for you, or doesn't care about you. He cares deeply about everything in your life. Literally, He knows the number of hairs on your head. There's nobody that's that close to you. No one else counts the amount of hair that comes out of your head. Especially women; He knows! He knows how many hairs are on your head! That's a God that cares and is in every detail of your life. I think sometimes we just get overwhelmed and we forget Who's with us, Who's holding us up, Who's holding our hand, Who's within us, and Whose power resides in us. We have the supernatural anointing of God residing in us! That anointing is so sharp, quick, and powerful. That anointing goes with you. It cuts through the atmosphere. It breaks through! So, what I want you to do is be bold and courageous, knowing that with the anointing of God, all the power that you need to resolve that situation or scenario is residing inside of you. And wherever you go, that anointing goes with you.

Do not be intimidated. Don't be overwhelmed. Don't be afraid. I want you to be bold and courageous, even if it's stepping out of the boat like Peter did and walking on water. Do it, and be bold and courageous about it! Are you willing to get out of the boat and walk and be bold and courageous, or have you been intimidated? Have you been overwhelmed? Have you allowed the fear of failure or disappointment or whatever it is to get a hold of you? No! You need to grasp right now that the anointing – the power of God – resides inside of you. That miracle-working power; that healing power; that creative power; that life-giving power; that breakthrough power; that deliverance power; whatever it is that you need, that is within you! It is holding your hand. It is upholding you and it never leaves you or forsakes you. You can't have God without His power. If you have God, you have His power. So you can be bold and you can step out courageously! Go ahead, speak it out of your mouth boldly because we're never going to see it if we don't believe, and we don't have faith, and we're overwhelmed, and we're intimidated, and we're discouraged, and we're dismayed.

God tells us over and over again. You want to know why He says it over and over again? Because He knows. He knows us. He knows human nature. He knows He needs to tell us over, and over, and over again. Sometimes fresh and new every single day. We need to be reminded of His power and that He is with us. That just makes me so happy. No matter what it is you go through; like Shadrach, Meshach, and Abednego being thrown into the fiery furnace, Isaiah 43 promises us that He will be with us in the fire. So no matter what it is you're going through, you might feel like, "Man there is nothing of God in this thing." Well, YOU carry God. You have God holding your hand, so it doesn't matter what the circumstances say, or dictate, or speak to your life if God is inside of you. God is holding you. You cannot fail. Come on! Be bold and courageous! I want you to speak forth the Word of the Lord that says nothing is impossible. Nothing is impossible to them that believe. *Literally,* nothing is impossible! Do you believe that? *Nothing* – that means that thing that you think is too tough, and too hard, or you're just intimidated by, that is NOT impossible for you! Be bold and courageous!

God is with you. It doesn't matter what we go through in life when we know that God is with us and nothing can harm us. With God going with us, what can be against us? Who can be against us with God on our side? Let's just take off that intimidation, that overwhelming, that feeling of being all alone, and that feeling of *I just can't do this*. NOPE. Maybe you can't, but guess what? The God inside of you *can*! Many times, I can't, and that's a true statement. Many times, I can't, but *every* time God can! God is inside of every single one of us. So rise up. Speak up. Be bold and courageous and step forward through that thing. Speak it out. Declare it, because God's holding your hand. He's holding you up. He goes before you. He's within you and He's gonna make it happen for you. Absolutely nothing – not one thing – is impossible for you.

Amen, and amen. You're not alone. God is with you. So shake that off! Shake off that intimidation. Shake off that fear. Shake off that doubt. Shake off that self-condemnation. Shake off that, "I'm all alone in this and I just can't do it" feeling. Shake that off and know that *nothing is impossible with God*.

Chapter 4
Fighting the Good Fight of Faith

So many people are fighting the good fight for faith. That's awesome! That's what God's Word tells us to do – fight the good fight of faith. But He also says *"My yoke is easy and my burden is light"* (Matthew 11:30). He's already won every single victory for you and that's why it's called fighting the good fight of faith. That's actually the only thing that we have to fight for is our faith. We don't have to fight for anything else. God has already done it. Everything that needs to be accomplished, He did it on the cross. He broke the power of sin. He broke the power of the curse of sickness on our lives and He was chastised for our peace. He was made poor so that we could be made rich. Every single thing has already been accomplished for us on the cross. That's why it's called fighting the good fight of faith. That's what we have to do, and it's the *only* thing we have to do.

We have to fight for our faith, trusting God no matter what we see, and no matter what we feel. We trust God. That's what he's talking about with fighting the good fight of faith. It is awesome and exciting that we know the outcome. We know the end. We know the result is victory, and that we win. So all we have to do is fight to keep standing and fight to keep believing. It's crazy that you can win this awesome, amazing victory, and then you think, "Oh well. My faith has got this I don't even need to worry about it anymore." No! In every single new thing that comes up, you're gonna need that faith, and every time your faith grows. But, just because your faith grows doesn't mean nothing's gonna come at you. I think so many times we step away from our faith because stuff happens and we think, "Oh well. It must be I'm just not a good enough Christian" or "They're just so much better than I am" or "God must be mad at me" or "This must mean He's not gonna do it for me and there's got to be a reason."

Absolutely not! That is when you fight the good fight of faith! I had a woman who's 71 years old come up to me and say "I just don't understand why I'm so weak in my faith because I still have things that I'm fighting." I told her, "The reason you've survived to 71 years old is because your faith *has* grown, and grown, and grown, and all you're doing is fighting the good fight." That's what you're doing is fighting the good fight, and it's a *good* fight.

His yoke is easy and his burden is light, and our fight is never against flesh and blood. There is no war against flesh and blood. It's against principalities and evil forces. That is the only fight that we have, and I want you to remember that! Take the face off that enemy. (Now I don't mean *take their face off*, but just remove the person's face from that fight.) It's not a fight against what you are going through, it's not a fight against that person. The Word of God says we fight against principalities and evil forces, and that's the only fight that we have. Fighting the good fight of faith is never against another person. The enemy of our souls wants you to put down your faith; wants you to get discouraged. That is the literal fight of the Christian. Because there is no other fight, you can't do anything more to accomplish what Jesus accomplished on the cross for you. In fighting the good fight of faith, faith is our shield (Ephesians 6:16). I love what the Word of God has to say. Look at Psalms 91:4-7. I want you just to hear this and see this:

"His massive arms are wrapped around you, protecting you. You can run under his covering of majesty and hide. His arms of faithfulness are a shield keeping you from harm. You will never worry about an attack of demonic forces at night nor have to fear a spirit of darkness coming against you. Don't fear a thing! Whether by night or by day, demonic danger will not trouble you, nor will the powers of evil be launched against you. Even in a time of disaster, with thousands and thousands being killed, you will remain unscathed and unharmed." Psalm 91:4-7 TPT

You will remain here right now. You are a child of God. You will remain unharmed and unscathed. That's fighting the good fight of faith. It's believing that above every circumstance, above every situation, you will be unharmed and unscathed. We see that in the scripture with Shadrach, Meshach, and Abednego (Daniel 3:19-27).

They went into the fiery furnace. Now listen – *legit* went into the fiery furnace. What about us Christians today? What would we say about them? "Ooooh," we say, "They must be doing something wrong. There must be something they're hiding. Oh, they're getting caught!" Absolutely not! They were fighting the good fight of faith. They were standing in the face of the enemy that was trying to steal, kill, and destroy. And when they did everything to stand, they stood, therefore, fighting the good fight. And guess what? They came out unharmed and unscathed!

The same thing happened with Daniel in the Lions' Den. We see it with Paul being shipwrecked. Just because something comes in and tries to trouble your life, it will not trouble you! It doesn't have to trouble you! That doesn't mean you're weak in your faith. Actually, it means the opposite. If you're fighting, it means you're growing your faith. You're getting stronger and better, and you're able to stand. And when you've done everything to stand, stand therefore! When you're praying and something isn't working out the way that you think it should work out, don't quit on your faith! Don't give up on your faith. That's the building of real faith.

It's not faith unless you have to use it.

If you don't have to utilize it and employ it, it's not faith. You don't even know what you've got until you have to stand. And when you've done everything to stand, *stand therefore*.

Now listen, do I believe bad things are gonna have to happen? Absolutely not. They don't have to happen. And if they do, they don't have to trouble you and you can come out unscathed. That's the point that I'm trying to make – even if bad things *do* happen, don't back out of faith!

Read Ephesians 6:11-17. This is where He gives us the armor of God. Why does He give you armor? It's for fighting the good fight! His armor is supernatural. It's not natural, it's *super*natural. In every battle, everything you're facing, everything you're fighting, in *every single battle*, take faith as your wrap-around shield (v16). I love The Passion Translation of this. Your faith right now is a literal wrap-around shield. I like to see it as a forcefield. I mean that's what wrap-around is; it totally encompasses you. It's like a supernatural force field that is around you. You have a supernatural forcefield! He says He's given us this armor to wear in every battle. In everything that you're facing,

"Take faith as your wrap-around shield for it is able to extinguish the blazing arrows coming at you from the evil one." (v16) That means there is a choice and an option. You have to choose: "What am I going to believe in this?" See, our only fight is for faith.

Faith is what you believe. What are you gonna believe? The Word of God says whatever you believe is what you are going to receive. We must fight to believe and stand in faith. Read the verse above again. You'll see it says, "it is able to" and that means if you choose to believe. If you choose to fight the good fight of faith, it will extinguish the blazing arrows coming at you from the evil one. Another version says, it will quench every fiery dart. That word *quench* means it will dissolve before it can penetrate; before it can hit you. So when you believe God above everything else, it doesn't matter what is slung at you – fire, lions, darts, words, sickness, disease, discouragement – it doesn't matter what's flung at you. That thing – it is able, if you choose to believe, to be extinguished before it even gets to you.

Listen, really bad things can have no effect on your life. No effect. I mean, literally, nothing can affect me except for that which I allow. That's the fight. Fighting the good fight of faith to stand, and when you've done everything to stand, stand therefore. When we live our lives within the shadow of God Most High, our secret hiding place, we will always be shielded from harm (Psalm 91:9-11). How then, can evil prevail against us or disease infect us? See, that's what our fight is. Our fight is to believe the Word of God above today's circumstances, above yesterday's circumstances, above our disappointments, and above the things that we saw before.

Are you going to believe this time? And that's where I really feel it is building our faith. It is the good fight of faith when we choose not to base what we believe about the Word of God on what we just saw, or what we saw yesterday, or what we saw happen with Aunt Susie or Lucy or Bill whomever. When we choose to believe, and stand, and stand therefore, *that* is the fight the good fight of faith. It goes on to say God sends angels with special orders to protect you wherever you go, defending you from all harm (Psalm 91:11). We need to commit these scriptures to our hearts because when we do, we're able to fight the good fight of faith and stand, and when we've done everything to stand, *stand therefore*.

Our faith is a shield to us. I love visuals because it helps me so much in realizing what's going on in my life. First of all, the shield of faith is protective. It protects me if it stops those fiery darts. It stops those attacks from even being able to get to me. They cannot penetrate, they cannot get in if I have my shield of faith up because the shield of faith says, "Whatever they say or do, this is what the Word of God says about it." He always has the truth, and He always has a promise. He always has a way of escape. His Word says it's for every single one who chooses to believe in Him.

So our belief is our faith, and our faith is a shield. It literally acts like a shield. So now every time you have to choose because he is able to work based on your belief.

Choosing fear keeps you completely exposed. I want you to hear me – it is keeping you completely exposed! Fear of "why didn't it happen this time?" or fear that maybe it won't happen this time because "look what already happened." That fear will keep you from being shielded, protected, and guarded, and all the while, He is able, He is able, He is able. But when we have our faith intact, it is the shield that will protect us. The Word says, "No weapon formed against me can prosper" and "Everything has to work out for my good." It doesn't matter what's going on around me. When I have my shield of faith up, it cannot affect my life. The shield of faith is not so you can cower behind it and be like, "Oh my goodness. I'm so afraid right now". Fear and faith don't work in the same place. It's either fear and you are exposed, or it's faith and you're shielded and guarded. So this shield is not so you can shrink back and go backward. The shield is so you can actually advance, even in the thick of it and in the worst onslaught of the battle, with things being launched from every direction. And that's what can happen when we have to fight the good fight of faith. We have to walk that out.

Sometimes we don't understand why things didn't happen and why God didn't show up like we thought He had to show up. We've been declaring and believing and it feels like that's the moment you're in the thick of this battle. God says "Advance, go forward, keep believing, and keep standing." In those moments, you have the shield so nothing can hurt you. You can advance in that time, in that moment, and get right through unscathed and unharmed. When we choose to fight the good fight of faith with our shields, it's to protect us, it's for advancement, and actually, it's much better than a physical shield that is just one-sided.

The Bible says we have a wrap-around shield, which means you have a forcefield around you. In 2 Kings 6:16-18, there was a battle where they were so outnumbered and it sure looked like they were surrounded and they were gonna die. But the man of God prayed that his assistant's eyes would be opened and he would see. When he opened his eyes, he saw spiritually that all of the angelic troops were surrounding them – absolutely surrounding them – and so, they were safe. That's what we need to see with our faith – that shield, that wrap-around, that army, those troops. There are more for you than are against you. Even in the thick of that, you need to know there are more for you than against you. You're fighting the good fight of faith! The shield is to protect you. It's for advancement. It's powerful. It's a forcefield. It is troops around you that way outnumber anything coming against you.

One of my favorite parts about the shield of faith is if I'm holding up the shield, I can't see my enemy! I can't see what they're doing. I can't see through it. I don't even know; therefore I am NOT reacting! It is not having any effect on me! I'm not on that rollercoaster ride. I can't even see it. I am walking in peace. This is the answer! This is the secret to fighting the good fight of faith – knowing I can't see what they're doing! And, I don't care what the enemy is doing because the Word of God says no weapon formed against you shall prosper (Isaiah 54:17). It says everything will work out for your good (Romans 8:28). We just read where it can't harm you. You will come out unscathed from the other side because of the shield of faith. But it is your fight! That's your fight – to hold the shield up in the middle of it. Hold it up when you start seeing and paying attention to what the enemy is doing; those darts being launched at you. If you do not have your faith shield up, I just want to warn you and I want you to hear me right. When you're seeing their actions and you're seeing the things that are coming against you and you do not have your shield up, you are exposed! It will rob you. You will not be able to stand. See, this is a choice that we have to make. When the shield is held up, you're not gonna know what they are doing, what they're saying, or what's happening. Every weapon formed will come to naught and it will quench any fiery dart. In every battle, *every* battle, *every single one.* No, this is not too big. No, this is not too hard. You have a shield of faith that will quench every fiery dart that comes in. God will protect you from everything. That's the fight that we have is to fight the good fight of faith.

I like to say, "Because I can't see, don't you dare come into my inner circle and tell me what the enemy is doing, because I have my faith shield up so I don't have to see what they are doing. You are not helping the cause by doing that. It's gossip, first of all — slander. It's unnecessary. Please don't tell me. Don't come back up in my safe place, and my place of peace in this easy yoke. Don't come in here and tell me what the enemy is doing against me. I don't care! It has no effect on my life. There's no effect on my peace, and has no effect on my advancement." It has no effect on *your* advancement! It has no effect on your next level unless you're putting your shield down. This is the only fight that we have is the fight the good fight of faith. That's why I call it a good fight. His yoke is easy and his burden is light (Matthew 11:30). It's not even a hard fight. It's not even against those people anyway. It's against principalities. It's not against flesh and blood.

And guess what?! Those principalities have already been defeated! He made an open show and a spectacle of them (Colossians 2:15). God's power surpasses the enemy's power so much that He flicks the enemy with his pinky finger! That very real, hard thing that you think is going to absolutely kill you because you're focused on it and you're seeing the enemy work? Put your shield up and know that His pinky finger flicks it off! That's exactly what it did! But we get ourselves so wrapped up in it. We get so caught up in the drama. We get caught up in the rollercoaster ride. No, just hold your shield of faith! I don't even see! Don't even look at it! If you see anything, see the angelic host of armies that are surrounding you right now, fighting for you! You cannot fail, you cannot fall! If you get knocked over, if something comes and knocks you down, you're still alive! *You are still alive!* That means you can continue to fight the good fight of faith. Your faith is your shield; your-wrap around shield! That's the only thing we need to fight for.

We need to be able to fight to stand in faith. And when you've done everything to stand, you keep standing! You keep believing. I don't care what comes. I don't care how bad it looks. It's always darkest before the dawn. Literally, the darkest time is just before the moment of breakthrough, just like Daniel in the lions' den and the Hebrew boys that went into the fiery furnace. I don't care what it looks like. I don't care if it looks like you are being thrown in that fire. Don't put your shield down! Fight that good fight of faith, child of God, because you're gonna come out the other side and escape. Who cares what anybody else says? Who cares what they say? Even if the other Christians say, "Oh there must be something going on in their life. There must be something bad. They must be hiding something. Oh, if we only knew what they were doing." Now listen you just keep standing! You hold that shield up and everything that comes in has to be quenched! It can't even get through that shield! Just fight the good fight of faith! That is all we have to do. It's easy; it is not hard. That is why it's called the good fight, because

He's already won! You're more than a conqueror (Romans 8:37); you're an overcomer (1 John 4:4). You're not just a conqueror, you're *more* than a conqueror because all you have to do is hold that shield up! The battle's already been fought and it's already been won. The devil's defeated. He's not even a contender in your life. The devil is the only enemy! That person, that thing, that scenario, that situation, that is not where the battle is. It's the enemy of your soul and he's already defeated. So take your mind off everything else, and put your eyes on the Word of God! Trust God and believe, no matter what! You see, no matter what happened yesterday, no matter what happened to anyone else facing the same situation; there are so many things that would love to come in and rob you of your faith. Don't let your faith be robbed!

The only fight you have in the Kingdom of God is fighting the good fight of faith. You will have what you believe. So that's what the Word of God says, but what happens when you really, really, *really* were believing for something and you didn't see it? This is where your faith grows. The disciples said, "Lord increase our faith" (Luke 17:5). This is where it's actually a fight to fight the good fight of faith. That's where we have to arrest our minds. I don't understand everything. I don't know why certain things happened. But it's not going to cause me to put my faith shield down, because then, I know it's not gonna happen. If I put my shield down, then I know the next battle isn't gonna be won. You need to sure up, even more, when you don't see it happen today. His ways are not our ways and His thoughts are not our thoughts (Isaiah 55:9), so we just have to trust God. Use that thing to catapult your faith to a whole new level. Take all the energy of disappointment from that thing and put it toward new faith! "Next time I'm just gonna lay hands on the sick person and see them recover. I'm not gonna cower back. I'm just gonna put all that energy into fighting the good fight of faith and believing above everything else what the Word of God says." That is the only battle that we have and that's the real one. It's real, it's absolutely legit that we have to believe God above our circumstances.

So, child of God, today get your shield up and fight that good fight of faith and advance! I'm telling you right now, I'm speaking and declaring advancement. Get up! Get up and walk through that situation. Stop allowing it to rob you of victory. Stop allowing it to rob you of increased faith. Stop allowing it to rob you of having that shield up. The enemy would love for you to do that; he'd love for you to put your shield down right now. NOPE! We're gonna advance right in. Advance and take ten steps forward today! I want you just to advance through! You have a shield. Whatever that awful, hard thing from the enemy that is facing you today is, I want you to take ten giant steps forward! You are so protected! You have a wrap-around shield. The victory has already been won for you. Do not allow fear – not even an ounce of fear. It is the good fight of faith. That is what we do. We fight the good fight of faith.

So, today, take ten giant steps and one of those first steps is not paying attention to what the other person is doing. Let's take that as our first giant step today. Hold that shield up so you don't even see what they're doing. Don't listen to what they're doing. Don't let anybody come in your bubble, in your space, in your forcefield, and tell you what the enemy is doing. You don't need to know because it has no effect on you. You're going through this unscathed.

Unscathed! It's going to work out for your good. It has no other choice. No weapon formed against you shall prosper. So whatever very real thing you're facing, we're taking ten giant steps right through the middle of that thing and coming out the other side!

Don't worry about your backside because you've got a wraparound shield. He's got your back. You don't have to worry about anything chasing you down or coming up behind you. You don't have those worries. It's not gonna sneak-attack, it's not gonna be an ambush because your faith is a wrap-around forcefield around you. So advance, advance, advance, advance, and increase your faith! This time the fight we have is for our faith, and it's easy. And our faith gets stronger and stronger every time we choose faith over fear; every time it gets stronger and stronger!

Chapter 5
It's a Life or Death Matter

We need to get back to the basics. Like, really just peel everything away. God is not complicated. It's not too hard or difficult. We just peel everything away and get back to the basics, because if we're not doing the basics, we're not advancing at all.

When you hear the scripture, don't just shut off and be like, "Well, yeah I know that, I hear that, I feel that. You know, I live that." That's one of the problems I think; we convince ourselves that we live these things. But I want to really break it down and look at it because when I heard this scripture the other day, something jumped inside of me. I thought, *You know, I think I do a pretty good job, but I probably could do a better job, and I definitely want to.* So, I want to talk about the power of the tongue and our words.

When we revisit this, I pray that it's a revelation for you too. I pray that when you hear this, it will be a revelation again, and just leap up inside of you and become alive. The scripture in Proverbs 18:21 tells us that the power of life and death are not in God's hands; they're not even in Satan's hands. Seriously, I know you've heard this scripture a whole bunch of times, but have you heard it with this reality – that the power of life and death have nothing to do with God?

He's done everything He can do. It has nothing to do with God, and it doesn't even have anything to do with Satan. The Word says that the power of life and death are in *your* tongue. Our tongue is where life and death reside. It has nothing to do with "God, I need you to show up! Oh, the devil's been beating me up." NOPE! The power of life and death is right here (I'm pointing at my mouth). It's in the words that we speak, and what we say out of our mouths. When I first heard this, I was like "Yeah, I really do a good job at that, but it's something that I want to do even better with." It's something that is so vital. It's so important. It's a life and death matter. Our tongue is a life and death matter. It's something that we should revisit and should really pay attention to.

I saw a certain social media post and then I was talking to somebody and they said the exact same thing the post said. So I know this is right on with God. The post I saw said, "Have you ever typed, and then deleted, then typed, deleted, and typed, deleted?" I think that's fresh for everybody right now, so I just know this is a Word that God is speaking and something that we need to pay attention to. We need to notice the words that come out of our mouths.

Psalms 39:1 AMP says, *"I said, I will take heed and guard my ways, that I may sin not with my tongue; I will muzzle my mouth as with a bridle while the wicked are before me."* Have you ever felt like that? Like you just needed to muzzle your mouth? Yes, absolutely. I saw somebody comment on that "type and delete" post that they need to do that with their face. Haha! You know what? I think this scripture covers that because if you put a muzzle on your mouth, it covers the whole facial expression too. So this scripture is about fixing your face and your tongue. Literally, we need to guard our mouths so much. It's like putting a muzzle on our mouths so we can't just say and do anything that we want to say and do. You can't just fly off at the mouth.

Listen, you are producing. When those words go forth, they are making something happen. What is it that they're making happen? The devil is just waiting for your words to come out. You know, maybe you've said the right thing and done the right thing. Guess what? The devil is waiting for that moment when you slip up, when you trip up, when you forget, or when you're not paying attention. He's waiting for you to let your guard down because you're saying, "Oh yeah, I do that. I'm not worried about it." No, we need to really focus and pay attention, and we need to muzzle our mouths. If you haven't felt the need to muzzle your mouth, I promise you, you're not doing a good job with this. Right there is the telltale sign. This is scripture; this is David speaking. He was a man after God's own heart and he had to muzzle his mouth. So, if we're not paying attention, we're not muzzling. And if you haven't felt the need to muzzle your mouth, you might be saying the wrong things. You might be saying things you don't want to say. You might be saying things that are just giving the enemy such juicy morsels to run with. He just gets so excited when you say those negative things, when you give in, when you're just like, "Oh, it doesn't really matter what I say." Yes, it does. It does matter! It matters that much! It is a matter of life and death. Every word you say out of your mouth is a matter of life and death.

Proverbs 30:32 AMP says, *"If you have done foolishly in exalting yourself, or if you have thought evil, lay your hand upon your mouth."* Psalm 141:3 says that our mouth is a door. Shut the door. Shut the door! You don't have to respond to every scenario. There is so much power in shutting the door and muzzling your mouth and laying your hand over your mouth. There's so much power in that.

Now, we can't *just* do that. You can't just be silent. You can't just say nothing, because we also have to create the path that we want to be walking into. We've got to create with our words. But we want to make sure that we are covering our mouths and not allowing any negative things to come out. Ephesians 4:29 is one of my all-time favorites. My kids had to write it and memorize it when they were younger. Whenever they said anything mean or bad, they had to write this scripture out ten times or twenty times, depending on what they said or how sassy they got about having to write it. It says, *"Let no corrupt communication proceed out of your mouth, but that which is good to use in edifying, that it may minister grace unto the hearers."* (KJV) Why? Why does God say that? Because it's a life and death matter, that's why He says it. We're not supposed to speak anything unless it builds encourages and edifies, and that's the Word of God. Not with your spouse, not with your BFF, not on your phone, and not on your Facebook feed. I know we can just get into that frustration mode and just blurt out and say whatever. That's when we need to just cover it. Shut the door. Muzzle it. Whatever you have to do to bite your tongue. The words that are coming out of your mouth are going to produce either life or death. There isn't any middle ground. There isn't a rollercoaster where it's just on cruise control. This is life or death. You are not designed to say things and expect something different. You are designed to speak things into manifestation.

Everything you are speaking is either going to bring life or death (Psalm 45:1 and Galatians 6:7-8). That's the best part! Let's get excited about the fact that your words can produce literal life in your situation! It can bring life. It can shift and change the atmosphere. It can cut through, and when we make our words His Word, it has to perform. It has no other choice. I get so excited about that part! I mean, yes, we have to be cautious and pay attention to the words that cause death. But I get even more excited that I have the power to create life in my own life with His words that do not return void! He cannot lie. It will accomplish what it is sent to do, and we can just stand. And when we've done everything to stand, you keep standing on the Word of God because the devil's waiting for you to think that his words or your own words or your own emotions are more powerful than the Word of God, *and they are not!* What makes you think that they are more powerful than the Word of God? You know, we do think they're more powerful, because we speak them out. And what we believe is what we actually speak. So we've got to make sure what we're believing is this, and no matter what your situation looks like, or how long you've been in it, don't change your confession! What's the alternative if you change your confession? You're just adding insult to injury. You're just adding ultimate death to that situation, that circumstance in your life. You're just adding that to it. Why not shift into believing the Word and what you speak will actually create life! It can change your cells. It can change your blood. It can change your health. It can change your financial position. It can change your relational positions. It's so much power. The power is in your mouth. It's in your words. It's not anything God can do.

I need to muzzle my mouth at times. Isn't it so true? I really try to pay attention to this. But when I was discussing this scripture with my husband, we were both like, "How do I do with that? Do I do okay?" "Yeah, you do well. You do well with that." But we still decided to hold each other accountable. Both of us said, "Well, you make sure you call me out. If you hear me say something, you correct me." It's great to have people that will hold you accountable. Don't be afraid to have people hold you accountable. If you are, that's just pride and that's keeping you from life. What kind of friend is it that would allow you to speak death, that would allow you just to be okay with death coming out of your mouth? You want a friend that's going to say, "Don't say that! You don't want to go there. That's probably not the right way to say it. Shut the door, shut the door!" No matter how they say it, it doesn't matter. If they say it nicely, or if they say it sharply, they should say it. And you should accept it, receive it, be accountable, and be okay with being accountable with your words.

If somebody helps you, be faithful to help other people. If you're hearing somebody speak death, teach them. Say, "Be careful because there's power in what you're speaking right now. You want to make sure you're speaking life and not death." You may say, "Oh well. It's just the truth. I'm just being real. I'm just speaking the truth." Really? It's truer than what God's Word says? That means you're not believing God's Word in the first place, so you're never going to see it happen if you're not believing the Word of God.

I love it when people say, "I'm just a realist." That's taking what's being served. That's taking the hand that you're dealt, and we don't have to do that. You don't have to take the hand that you're dealt. Isn't that so exciting? You can say, "Nope. This is what the Word of God says – that He'll prosper me and He will keep me. He'll restore me. He'll give me all the wisdom." Whatever it is you need, God has it for you. That's what I'd rather believe than whatever "seems" real or whatever's been dealt to me in this life. Be cautious of even thinking, *I'm just being real about the situation.* No, the most real thing is the Word of God. The most real thing is God Himself.

In Job 6:24, Job is speaking to the Lord. Remember all those bad things that happened to Job? It wasn't the Lord. The Lord didn't do those things to him. Actually, what it says is the thing that Job feared the most came upon him (Job 3:25-26). So, it came upon him because he was afraid, and we're not supposed to be afraid. Don't even talk about whatever that thing is that you fear the most! Not in your words or your thoughts or in the meditations of your heart! That's what happened to Job, and guess what? When Job got a hold of this, when he got a hold of his tongue, that's when everything turned around for his good! That's when everything changed. Remember when he was commiserating with his friends? It didn't do anything for him.

Everybody likes to go to Job, so I'm just going to go with that. If you so enjoy using Job for your misery, then use the same thing for your victory, because Job shut his mouth! And when he declared the Word of the Lord, that's when everything changed! So if you're in that boat of, "Oh Job, Job, Job, Job, the misery of Job," I want you to jump on board with, "Well, when he covered his mouth and he started speaking right according to the Word of God, things broke loose! That's when they started shifting. That's when they started changing. So his words produced death, and the same mouth spoke words that then produced and caused life." Job 6:24 KJV says "'Teach me, and I will hold my tongue; and cause me to understand wherein I have erred.'" This was what he was saying – his error was in his words. It was in what he had spoken. Then he decided to speak the truth; to speak the Word of God.

I know it's a cliche, and we hear this all the time, and you're like, "Yeah, yeah, yeah, I know. The power of life and death." I just want to remind you again because it's super easy in this atmosphere that we're in; in society right now, to give in to frustration and to give in to emotions. Maybe you've just been dealing with something for a long time. Maybe you're giving in to time. I'm just reminding you that those words you speak, they are powerful! They are either life or death and you can turn your situation around right now with what you say and with what you do. Our words are so important.

I'm not here preaching at you. I'm sharing what God's working on in me. A lot of times I find when talking to people that God is speaking to everyone on the same thing. So, let's hear Him! Let's be hearers of the Word. But, let's not be hearers only. It's great to hear a Word and say "Oh, that's so good." But let's be *doers* of the Word! I want you to start speaking life over those circumstances, and those things that are frustrating you. Things that have gotten you discouraged, and that have gotten you angry; things that depress you and make you sad. I want you to start speaking the truth of the Word of God over that and watch – just watch! You know, it might take standing, and when you've done everything, to stand therefore, but God cannot lie! His Word is the greatest truth. It is the greatest power. Greater is He that is in you than He that is in the world (1 John 4:4). There is more power inside of you than anything you're ever going to face. So, let's watch our words.

Sometimes we say little cliche things like, "Oh, you're killing me." Those seem like just little things. We have to be so cautious of what our words are directing and what they're making happen in our lives because words are making things happen. They're either making good things or bad things happen. I promise you the devil is just waiting. He is going to ride those negative words. He's going to ride depression. He's going to ride fear. Just like he did with Job; he waited for those words to come out and he rode them and he brought such destruction, devastation, and death to Job's life. But when your words are life and the Word of God, they are going to produce life. So be cautious of the things you say, and don't give up on those right things and those good things. Don't let your guard down for a moment because the devil is waiting.

Why would you give up? Why would you throw in the towel? At no point will I do that. I will not. I can tell you this from experience because my life has not been perfect (silver platter, bed of roses, lollipops, gumdrops, rainbows, fluffy clouds, etc.). But I can tell you from experience, that at no point will I give my words over to the enemy. There is no point when I will give up. What for? It will only allow it to be worse, and you don't need worse. You don't need worse, what you need is to continue to speak life. Continue at all costs. Continue at all times to speak life and to speak words that are going to create life for you, because the alternative is no alternative at all! It's not an option. It's not an option at all. We want our words to stay true to the Word of God because it is more powerful. The Word is more powerful than anything and everything you will ever face. Even with trouble, because of the words I've chosen to speak with my mouth, my life has been full of joy, peace, abundance, strength, overcoming, and victory.

Stay on guard at the door of your tongue. Muzzle it. Put your hand over it if you have to. Do whatever you've got to do, but make sure you're speaking life and not just over other people. Make sure you also speak life over yourself. "Oh, I'm just so dumb." NO! Don't ever speak those things. "Oh, that was so stupid." Don't speak those things. Duct tape, maybe? I know sometimes you have to try to put the negative things back in your mouth when they start coming out. ("Get it back in there!") Just be so cautious and don't be afraid again. Don't be afraid to get other people to put you in check, and when they do (especially if it's your husband), don't yell at them and don't get mad at them, even though it will feel like you should get angry about it. Allow them to correct you, because this is a life and death matter. Seriously, it is a *life and death matter*. So make sure you're guarding your words at all times and never let your guard down. Never give up on your words and your declarations because it matters. It matters and it's so super important. I pray that you'll be a doer and not just a hearer only and that you'll start creating life with your words and building a life that you want to walk in with your words. Because when the Word goes forth – especially when we're standing on this – it has to perform. It has no other choice and again, it's not up to God.

It's up to you and me.

Chapter 6
Get Up, Dress Up, and Show Up

One of my mottos in life is to "Get up, Dress up, and Show up." It is so important; especially in the moments of feeling like you don't want to. Like you'd rather just throw on your sweatpants and sweatshirt. It's easy today (because you don't even have to leave your house) to just not get up, dress up, and show up. It's so important to do it, though! Get up, dress up, and show up, *no matter what*! No matter if you feel like it or not – get up, dress up, and show up. During this time when it's easy to not dress up, we need to still be getting up, dressing up, and showing up to our day. This is especially true if you're married. If you're married, get up and dress up. Take a shower! It's kind of important! So, we need to make sure that we're showing up when we need to.

This is a great tactic against the enemy because if he doesn't get to see the effect that he's having, we can trick him. We can let him think he's not getting to us. It's so important to not let him get to us; not let him get in there and think that those jabs that he's delivered have taken effect. I love not letting the enemy see my weakness when he is coming in for an attack. I won't let him see me in those moments of, "I just don't feel like it" because he will take advantage of that. It'll be one of those "Maybe this time" situations. He's thinking, "Maybe this time they're not up, they're not ready, they're not dressed, and they don't feel it. I can see they don't feel like it, so I'm gonna take advantage of this opportunity. I'm gonna get in there and I'm gonna throw some jabs at them." I never want to give the enemy that opportunity or that foothold. I don't want him to see when I'm struggling or when I'm feeling weak because – let me tell you – he is dirty! He plays dirty and he will take complete advantage of you showing how you're feeling by not getting up and dressing up.

Romans 13:14 in The Message version literally says, *"Get out of bed and get dressed!"* I love that! Get out of bed and get dressed no matter how you feel about it. Get out of bed and get dressed. It goes on to say, "Don't loiter and linger, waiting until the last minute. Dress yourself in Christ and be up and about!" That's the whole slogan right there – get up, dress up, and show up. I just thought that was hilarious when I read it. I was like "Man, I've been saying that for years. I've just been quoting the Word of God." It's so true, especially when we're dealing with the enemy.

Another reason why we need to get up, dress up, and show up is that we always need to be ready. Matthew 25:1-13 is the parable of the wise and foolish virgins. The ones that got up, dressed up, and showed up were prepared and ready. They were the ones that were there when Jesus came back. The ones that didn't get up, dress up, and show up weren't prepared, and guess what? They didn't get to go with Him! That's a big deal! That's life! I'm talking about *eternal life*! It's not just this no-big-deal thing! No! We've got to get up, dress up, and show up so that the enemy doesn't get to see that he can get in. If you show him one sign of weakness — go ahead, you keep those sweatpants on, you keep that sweatshirt on, don't comb your hair, don't get ready — he's coming in like a lion seeking whom he may devour and he's gonna be merciless.

So we've got to pay attention to what we allow him to see in our lives. This has always been a tactic that I love using against the enemy. He will never, ever see me flinch. He has enough ammunition against us already, I will never give him a foothold in my life. I will never let him see any kind of weakness in me at all because I know he's gonna come in and jab those spots and try to take me out. So, it is imperative in our fighting the good fight of faith. It is *imperative* that you get up and put yourself together. What does it say in Romans? It says get out of bed and get dressed. Don't loiter and linger, waiting until the last minute. Dress yourself in Christ and be up and about!

Get up and about no matter what your day has for you; no matter if there's nothing planned and nothing on the agenda, and it's the same old, same old, ho-hum day. Guess what? Get up, dress up, don't loiter, and don't wait until the last minute. Dress yourself in Christ and be up and about. It's the Word of God (Romans 13:14)! I challenge you to read through The Message version. It's just really a cool version to use when you read this passage and Matthew 25 about the wise and foolish virgins. It says the Kingdom of Heaven shall be likened unto ten virgins who took their lamps and went out to meet the bridegroom. Now five of them were wise and five were foolish. Those who were foolish took their lamps and took no oil with them; but the wise took oil in their vessels with their lamps. While the bridegroom was coming, the ones that didn't bring oil had to go out and try to find oil for their lamps. So we need to be ready for the Lord when He has something for us. We need to be ready for His return. We have to be paying attention! It says He will come like a thief in the night when you're not expecting it (1 Thessalonians 5:2). So, we've got to be ever-expecting. We've got to be ever-ready for the Lord to return.

We also have to be ever-ready for whatever mission God has for us. If you're lying around in your sweatpants and sweatshirt and you can't get up out of bed, when He has something for us to do (which He always has), we're not ready. We are supposed to be ambassadors for Christ and we're lounging around in sweatpants and a sweatshirt and haven't even combed our hair? If He says, "I need you to go do this," you can't be like, "Well God, I'm not ready. I can't do that right now because look at me. Have you seen me?" We have to get up, dress up, and show up so that we're ready for everything that God has for us to do as His ambassadors. We've got to be ready at any moment.

If we are going to get through the fire, we must take action. I'm talking about having tenacious faith that moves you. If you're not happy with where you're at, with what's going on, with your circumstances, with all of those things; and if they're not changing, you've gotta get your faith and get up and move yourself out of that position. It's not going to change until you move yourself out of that position. We're gonna stay right in the place we're at unless we move with our faith, up and out of that position. We have got to! This is a call to action! We have got to do something different.

You know, I think culture has lulled people into a way of doing things. A way they didn't *want* to do things, but yet, they conformed. It just happened and now you're in this place. Maybe it's a doctor's report that you are given and it's not changing. You have to be the one that gets up and moves yourself through. Get yourself up out of that position. When the disciples came to the lame man, Jesus actually said pick up your bed and walk. *Pick up your bed and walk!* Right now I'm telling you, pick up your situation— get up! Get up out of your situation and walk. It's not going to change as long as you lay there, as long as you sit there, as long as you keep that same mentality and that same thought process. It's going to take tenacious faith for you to shake yourself loose of that and that's what you have to do. If we don't do anything different, nothing is going to change. Hear me, *we have the power!* This is not advice. This isn't even something that you *should* do. The Word of God tells us we *must* change.

In Romans 12:2, it says, *"Don't be conformed to this world but be ye transformed."* We have got to be transformed. Our thinking has to be transformed. It has to be renewed. Whatever you put in the most is what's going to take root in your life. You're in the Word of God an hour or two hours a day and for the rest of your day, all of this other stuff is being filtered in. So we have got to take control over our lives and be transformed by the renewing of our minds. In the New Living Translation, Romans 12:2 says, *"Don't copy the behaviors and customs of this world."* We have got to shake ourselves out of it, but let God transform us. If you don't like where you're at; if you don't like this position; if you're not happy with what's going on around you, transform yourself! You have the power to transform your circumstances and your situation. It says, *"Let God transform you into a new person by changing the way you think then you will learn to know God's will for you…"* God's will for you is that you have life, and life more abundantly (John 10:10). If you're not in that right now, get up! Get up out of that position. Get up out of that doctor's report. Get up out of that sickbed. Get up out of that circumstance. Get up out of that bitterness. Get up out of that hatred. Get up out of that offense. Get up out of that unforgiveness. Get up out of that way of thinking; that way of doing things. It's just kind of happened to you, but you need to get up out of it right now!

This isn't a time for soft Christianity. I'm sorry, but if you have soft Christianity, I'm praying for you. I'm not going to say you're not going to make it, because I'm not going to speak that over your life. I'm saying I'm praying for you. If you've got soft faith, if you've got weary faith, if you've got tired faith, I am praying for you because this is gonna take *tenacious* faith! It's gonna take you getting up, getting your faith, and marching right up out of that. Pick up your bed and walk! It's not going to change unless you do.

Psalm 23 says, *"Yea though I walk through the valley of the shadow of death I will fear no evil for you are with me."* Did you hear that? It says "Yea though I walk through the valley of the shadow of death." *Through, through,* I walk *through.* You're not supposed to sit down and park there! We're not supposed to stay in this mindset. We're not supposed to stay in this thinking. We're not supposed to stay in that place. Whatever has interrupted your race – and this *is* a race – run the race to win! Paul says this isn't "lazy boy" Christianity. Get up and get moving! You don't want to sit down in that place. You don't want to stay in that place. You certainly don't want to dwell in that place! It says, "Yea though I walk through the valley of the shadow of death." If you're parking there, if you got your lazy boy chair in that place, if you're stuck in that place, that's not where you want to be! You want to be going *through.* Where Jesus is, is going through! He's taking you through the fire, and you will not be burned!

This doesn't mean there's not gonna be fire. There's gonna be fire! That happens, especially if you stand up for God. But listen, don't be afraid of that! He says even though there's trouble in the world, don't you dare be afraid, don't you cower, don't you shrink back in that place because He's already overcome the world (John 16:33). He has deprived it of its power to harm you! You've got to renew your thinking right now. You've got to transform it.

How do we do that? With the Word of God. You've got to grab hold of the Word of God like never before. Quote the Word of God over your circumstance, over your situation, over what you are going through, and get up and get out of that mindset! Get out of that sickbed, get out of that doctor's report, get out of that bad place, get out of that negative place, get out of that depression, get out of that fear right now in the Name of Jesus! Get out of that anxiety. It's gonna take action on your part. Get up, pick up your bed, and walk right out of that circumstance. He's given you the authority. Luke 10:19 tells us He's given us authority that nothing by any means – *by any means* – coming in can harm you. Unless of course, you sit back and you stay in that place and you let that place overtake you.

Trust me, I know what I'm talking about. I know what it takes to have to have faith, and when you've done everything that you could do to stand, to stand therefore. But listen to me, God takes you through. You don't get stuck, you keep moving. You keep advancing. You're not even gonna smell like smoke! He who began a good work in you is going to complete it until the very end (Philippians 1:6).

You get out of that place that you're in right now. You are not in a stuck place unless you've parked yourself. This soft faith isn't cutting it! It is impossible to please God without faith, and faith without works is dead. *Faith without works is dead.* There's nothing to it. Your faith requires action and if you're not taking action, that's why it's not changing. The scenery is not changing because you haven't taken action against it. I know things happen that are out of our control, but I'm shaking you and saying, "Take some action with your faith!" Get up out of that circumstance. Bring yourself up out of it! Transform your mind. Renew it with the Word of God. You've got to make it happen. It is not going to change unless you change it. Sitting back and just praying cute prayers and rocking in your rocking chair isn't going to cut it! You *have* to act! God has already done everything that He needs to do. You've been given everything that you need to succeed for life, for godliness, everything has already been done. The only requirement is for you to act, for you to get up, for you to change the way you're speaking, to change the way you're thinking, to change what you're doing.

I know maybe things shut down, maybe you stopped doing things, and maybe you've been isolated, and maybe you're all alone. Change it! Change it by getting up out of that place! The Word of God tells us to not forsake the assembling of ourselves together (Hebrews 10:25). It's the Bible. It's the Word of God. Get together with people. It's what you are created to do. You weren't created to hibernate in your home. But you're the only one that has the power to change your circumstance. It's not a suggestion, and it's not God's advice.

In the Word of God, Romans 12:2 tells us to be transformed. So right now I'm telling you, God is saying to you, "Be transformed" out of that place. "Be transformed" out of that thinking. Anything that raises itself up against the Word of God is not where you're supposed to be stuck. It's not supposed to be where you're dwelling. It's not supposed to be where you're thinking. It's not supposed to be where you're meditating. So right now, if you want to see it change, change it! You have the power in your words, in your hands, in your feet, in your actions, and in your thoughts. You are the one who's gonna have to change this. God isn't gonna pick up your shield for you. He's not gonna pick up your armor. *Come on*, toughen up! It's gonna take tenacity! Pick up your bed, pick up your shield, get out there and start advancing in the Kingdom of God. You've got to move forward. You've got to move out of this place. You've got to move from that stuck mentality. You've gotta move out of that negativity. You've gotta move out of that isolation! Come on — it's in *your* hands!

You've been empowered to take action today. Shake yourself off. You don't want to be left behind. You don't want to be weak in your faith. I think that we have just been so blessed that there has been complacency. And anytime we face anything hard, all we've done is crumble. This is not the time or the season. When you're in a race and you get toward the end, that's not when you kick it into neutral. That's not when you start relaxing. No, these are the end times! The Word of God tells us very clearly the signs of the end times. If ever there were signs, we are now seeing signs of the end times! You are not in the first leg of the lap where you just kind of pace yourself. We are not in a *pace yourself* part of the race right now. We're at the end of the race. This is where you've gotta dig down deep with everything that's in you and pull yourself up by your bootstraps and push with everything that you've got in you! The Bible tells us to run the race to win (1 Corinthians 9:24). That means you gotta come out fighting. That means you gotta come out standing, and when you've done everything to stand, you dig even deeper and you just keep standing. You keep pressing in.

If you've built yourself on the rock, Matthew 25 tells us you are on solid rock and not on sinking sand. Stop that mentality right now! Tell yourself "I'm not on sinking sand." I don't care if everything caves in around me, the thing I can guarantee you is I will still be standing! I will still be standing because the Word of God tells me if I build myself on the rock, then the winds can blow, the rain can pour on me, and the floodwaters can even overtake me, but guess what? I will still stand in the midst of all of it. Listen, Christian; listen, child of God – shake yourself right now! Take yourself out of that complacent place that you've been in; that fearful place, that stuck place, and that discouraged place. You are the head and not the tail. You win, you win, *you win*!

We know the end of the story. Victory is ours. It's already been purchased for us with the precious blood of Jesus. To me, that is enough. Nothing is bigger than the precious blood of Jesus that overcame everything. Your condition is not more special than the price that Jesus paid on the cross. Oh please — come on — the devil has lied to you. There's nothing greater or stronger than the precious blood of Jesus! There is nothing greater than the power of the Almighty. His power is surpassing anything and everything that you will ever face. This is the transformation that needs to happen. I'm giving you the Word of God. I'm giving you an infusion of the Word of God right now. Victory is yours! You will win. I don't care how long it's been dark. I don't care how long it's been scary. I don't care how long you've been alone. I don't care how long it hasn't changed. You win in the end. God is gonna work it out for your good. He who began a good work in you is going to complete it until the very end. You can't be a complacent, soft Christian. It is not the time and season for that. The Word of God tells us to pay attention to the seasons. There may have been a season when we could sit back and enjoy the blessings of God. Let me tell you, in adversity, the blessings of God shine all the greater on the children of God! When there's famine, the children of God are blessed. When there's adversity coming at us, we can't cower and we can't bend. We can't be blown over by everything that comes our way. That's not faith at all. Faith is when something comes at you, you actually stand. You may have faith, but it's only a theory until it's actually tested. If your faith's being tested, you win this!

The end of the story is that you're a victor. The end of the story is that you win. The end of the story is that you will still be standing. Don't you dare stay down in that sickbed. Don't you dare stay in that fear. Don't you dare stay in depression. Don't you dare stay in anxiety. Don't you dare stay in those circumstances. Get yourself up and walk right out of it, right now, in the Name of Jesus! That's what you've been authorized to do. You've been authorized to go right into that fire and stand there. Jesus is standing right there with you. You're not being burned up. You are not being scalded. You aren't even smelling like smoke. Come on — toughen up! You need to have tenacious faith.

I'm speaking over you right now. God is giving an infusion of faith for you. Maybe you feel like you've been depleted of everything you had just to get through this. Guess what? His mercies are brand new every morning! He's bringing you from faith to faith, and from glory to glory. He's gonna give you the strength that you need. You are not weak. You are not weak, and you are not too tired. He's gonna give you supernatural strength! He's gonna give you what you need for every single day, fresh and new. If you deplete everything that you have, if you push so hard, and you have so much tenacious faith in today, guess what? Tomorrow it's brand new strength, brand new faith, and a brand new fight! That's the beautiful part of our God! You don't deplete yourself. As we give out, He gives in. Give and it shall be given unto you, pressed down, shaken together, and running over (Luke 6:38). When you've given everything you've got, give! Go ahead and give everything you've got because it's going to be pressed down, shaken together, running over, and given unto you. You're going to get more, and more, and more. That is the beautiful part about being a child of God; we don't ever get depleted. You're never depleted. That is a lie from the devil. That is a lie from the enemy. Stop believing it. God's Word clearly tells us that as we give, it's gonna be given back into us, pressed down until it's completely running over. You are not too tired. Stop saying it. Stop buying into it. Stop believing it! It's a lie from the enemy.

God energizes us. He infuses us with the strength that we need for everything that we are going to face. My prayer is that you will be infused with a tenacious faith. But that's going to require you to take action. Get up! Get up and walk out of that place. Walk right through it and don't cower at it. Nothing shall, by any means, harm you. Nothing.

The devil cannot kill you. He can do all manner of stuff and try to get you flustered, but that's what he's counting on. The devil is counting on "maybe this time."

You know, you may have had great victories in the past and now all this stuff has happened to you. It's coming from every angle and every avenue. The enemy is counting on this time being the time that you give up; the time that you give in. God has never forsaken the righteous. Not once. He will not forsake you. He will never leave you or forsake you. That's what it says. Not this time and not any time. Don't buy the lie of the devil that this time's just too much and that this time it's not going to change. That's a lie from the enemy.

When Jesus was in the wilderness and He was being tempted by the devil, He was hungry. He was alone. He had been out there in the wilderness and He was at the most possible weakest, physical point. And that's when the devil came in to tempt Him. You know what? He won! He won with the Word of God. It says at the end of that, that the devil didn't run away forever. No, he went just far enough off, waiting for a more opportune time (Luke 4:13). Don't let this be his more opportune time in your life. He can never win against you unless you drop your sword, unless you drop your shield, unless you just sit down and stay in that place. He can't win against you. Don't let this be his "Maybe this time they're gonna give up." "Maybe this time when it doesn't change." "Maybe this time when it comes in from all angles." "Maybe this time when it's too scary." "Maybe this time when it's too dark." "Maybe this time." "Maybe this time." That's what he's counting on. Don't give in to the devil! He loses. He does not win unless you hand the victory over to him.

So, get up! Get your tenacious faith and you change and transform your circumstances right now. Walk in the power of Almighty God right through that situation. Have so much faith that people look at you and say, "Wow! How on earth is this happening? It's not even possible that they're in the fire and they're not being burned up." That's your story. *That's yours!* Don't let the devil write your story. Don't let circumstances, and don't let life write your story. *You* get to write your story with the Word of God and the power of God. *That's* your story. You win! You'll still be standing. But it's going to take action — tenacious faith. So get up and get going!

We have to be ready for His return. We have to be ready for whatever mandate He has. We have to be ready and watching, making sure the enemy is not going to come in and attack us when we're off guard. Get up, dress up, and show up. It's simple, quick, and easy, but you actually have to do it. I'm encouraging you – every day, get up, dress up, and show up, no matter what your agenda has for the day. Because God has an agenda for you. Guess what? The enemy has an agenda for you, too! We have got to be paying attention to him at all times. Write those scriptures down. Romans 13:11-14 and the entire chapter of Matthew 25 are about being ready. We've got to be ready. So get dressed. Get ready for whatever mission God has for you today. He's got something for you to do, and for you to accomplish. It might not even be leaving your house, but it might be. He might say, "You need to FaceTime So-and-So" or "So-and-So might be FaceTiming you." And you'd be like, "No, no. I can't answer that FaceTime. Have you seen me?" We need to be ready – ever-ready.

So get up, dress up, and show up! You have a mandate from the Lord and you have an enemy that's hoping he can catch you while you're down. I'm praying that, through the Word of God, you're gonna be ready and vigilant like those wise virgins. So when the Lord comes, and when the enemy shows up, you're ready for either, and you're ready for the mandate that God has for you.

Chapter 7
Maintaining the Garden of Our Lives

What do I mean by that? It's like the thorns, and the thistles, and the rocks and the weeds that grow up in the garden. It's the same thing with our lives.

Each day, you have to pay attention to what you're putting in, how you're receiving and responding, and how you're tending to that ground. Also, you need to pay attention to what you're allowing each day and what you're removing and taking out. We have to be constantly aware and paying attention. The hard thing about a garden is that it's actually work! It's actually work, so most people avoid even doing a garden because it's work. Let's not avoid tending to our lives because it is work to pay attention to those things that are cropping up and what we're purposing to put into our lives. I mean, realistically, that's the most important thing. If we purpose what we're putting in (for example, we're putting in enough of the Word of God to get saturated in it, praise, prayer, and powerful sermons on the Kingdom of God), then you don't have to worry because it's all just being overtaken with good things.

But a garden is hard to tend to. We have got to pay attention. It isn't something that you can just neglect. We can't neglect tending to our own lives, our own emotional states, and offenses that come up. Offenses come up all the time. You're going to get offended more than once a day, and you have to make sure you're attending to that. You have to be weeding, throwing stones out, not holding on to offenses, forgiving quickly, letting things go, and making sure that your life is free from those things. Those things can stop the fruit from appearing. There's a purpose in tending to our gardens because when we tend to them, we will produce fruit, and we all want our lives to produce fruit. But if we're not tending to the garden, we just get caught up with the busyness of life. We can get caught up with the anxiety of life when we're not tending the garden. We're allowing those thorns and weeds and we will not be fruitful. It is imperative that we pay attention to maintaining the garden in our own lives.

Just because weeds and thorns and rocks come up doesn't mean you're doing anything wrong. It's just normal. My parents had a garden when I was younger but they didn't tend it; us children got to tend to that garden. I'm telling you, if we skipped a day, if we were like, "You know what? We don't need to do it today, we did it yesterday," oh, my goodness; it made it so much more work the next day!

It is amazing how those weeds grew! But it wasn't because we did anything bad that the weeds were there, or that the rocks would come up. It was just normal. It just happened. We just have to pay attention to maintenance. Just because you are feeling like, "Man, I'm always pulling these weeds. Man, I'm always overcoming these offenses. Every single day I'm pulling out these rocks," doesn't mean there's something wrong with you. It's quite normal for your life and for a garden to have those rocks.

Jeremiah 4:3 says break up your fallow ground and do not sow among thorns. This is telling us we have got to pay attention to the ground in our gardens. Hosea 10:12 tells us the same thing; break up your unplowed ground. Mark chapter 4 and Luke chapter 8 are all about the types of ground that people live in: stony ground, rocky ground, hard ground, thorny ground, weeds, and all those things. He tells us that we need to keep our lives free of all of those things, and the way we do that is by maintaining our gardens daily.

Don't let a day go by! We can't wait until, "Oh, I have to teach a class so I better study." No, this is about your ground and maintaining your own ground. You need to be in the Word of God, plowing. The Word of God just plows that ground. It breaks it up. It breaks up anything that goes crosswise from the Word of God. When you put the Word of God in, it will break up all of that foul ground, all of that hurt, and all those hard places. So, we've got to make sure we're maintaining the ground of our lives, and that we're paying attention. There are going to be things that are said today that could cause fear, that could cause anxiety, that could cause pain, hurt, offense, that could cause you to just feel strangled by the weeds and poked at by the thorns. There are going to be things that come up. Are you just going to allow those things and accept those things or are you gonna weed those out and say, "No, I'm choosing to pull that out and not participate with that in the ground of my life"?

I want the ground of my life to be so pure and so fertile that I'm able to produce fruit in every area of my life. We want to be productive. We want to see God move. We want to see His Word not return void. But that responsibility is on us. His Word is powerful and it's true, but if you're planting His Word in stony ground, it is a law of nature, science, and the Kingdom of God, that it *cannot* produce. It won't happen. We have got to make sure we're not getting caught up in the daily anxiety and distraction and busyness and forgetting. These things that are coming up, we have to tend to them. We have to take time to root it out. Sometimes these things that look so small have some seriously deep roots inside of them. They've been building up there for a while and then it just pops out on the surface and it looks like nothing. But it's more than something, it's got some deep roots that you have to dig down and get. We do that with the Word of God, with praise and exalting Him, lifting Him up, and magnifying God over all those things all the time. None of those things, no matter how deep the root, is greater than the God that you serve. We need to be continuously praising God. That's how you get those deep-rooted things, those hard things, and those massive rocks that come to the surface out. They come out by you just praising God!

We bought a house that had no grass. It was just dirt and stones. We did all the work ourselves. Back when we didn't have anything, we had to do all of the hard labor on our own. It's good and it builds character. It trains you in the things of God and in spiritual things. We can apply it today to spiritual things, but we have to pick up those rocks. We would clear an area. We would just focus on one little area. We'd clear it out and then move to the next area, clear it out, and then, you know what's crazy? We'd wake up the next day and there would be more rocks in that area! It's just a natural part of life. Things are going to come up in your life. Hard places are going to come up in your life. What do you do? Do you just leave it there? No! You get in! Maybe you need some help. Maybe it's going to take two people. Sometimes I couldn't lift those rocks myself. I had to get somebody else to come over and help me lift that rock and chuck it out. But we've got to daily maintain in our lives.

If we aren't cutting them off, if we're not taking captive

every single thought, it's so easy for weeds of negativity to just get in our thoughts and in our minds. Trust me, I know how easy it is. It's real. It's in your face. It's your life. We need to treat it even more seriously *because* it is real and *because* it is our lives. You can't let your guard down on that garden at all or it's gonna be an overwhelming process to get all of those weeds cleaned up. It's gonna be more work in the future to get those things cleaned out, so pay attention to them today, right now, when they come up. Do you take those thoughts captive when they come up? Arrest them when they come up? Don't allow them to get deep roots in there. Don't allow them to grow to the surface. Sometimes a rock, a small rock, when it starts surfacing, you're like, "Oh, you know that's not that big." Then you realize, "Oh my goodness! That was just a little knob on the rock, now there's a whole big massive rock underneath!" We've got to be maintaining the garden of our lives on a daily basis. It is so important because when those things come in, when those hard times come, in those hard places, when those thorny times come, and when those weeds try to choke us out, they can overtake us.

If we haven't paid attention, if we're not maintaining, it is too difficult and you will be overtaken. That is not God's desire for any one of us. He wants us to have abundant life and life more abundantly. He wants us to walk with ease, but we've got to follow His plan and His purpose. That's forgiving. That's not being offended, being anxious for nothing, and having no fear! It's so easy for us to just shake them off as just normal things or think, "I must be doing something wrong." No! We've got to pay attention. Maintain your garden every single day so that when you need the fruit, when you need to be producing, you'll be able to produce. If you have not maintained your garden and you need to produce fruit in a situation, nothing can grow in stony ground. Nothing can grow in those weeds and thorns. It cannot produce fruit. We have got to maintain daily. Maintain those things. Don't let them get a stronghold on you. Don't let the enemy get a foothold. Don't crack the door for him, because once we do, it's just like a weed.

The enemy is just like a weed; it will overtake everything in just moments. We've got to be on guard! We've got to pay attention and maintain our lives so we can be producers and we can have fruit coming from our lives. It's too easy to get lazy, to just get relaxed. We can never get to that place. Jesus is coming back soon and we can't afford to be having stony, weeds, and thorns filled with anxiety and fear. We can't afford to have that in our lives. We've got to keep them maintained so that we can walk in the power and produce for the kingdom of God.

I just pray that this has been a good reminder for you to maintain every single day. Sometimes you might have to do it multiple times a day. Remember, it doesn't mean that you're a bad person because these things are happening; it just means you're alive and you're in this world. You have the power to maintain and it's much easier when you maintain daily than when you let it go. Let's get to maintaining daily! Get in the Word of God. Praise God. Praise God in the storm. Praise Him, and when you look out and you see that weed cropping up, starting to choke things out, just praise God! Get in His word. Build yourself up! I can't even stress the importance of building yourself up enough. Build yourself up in the most holy faith. The Word of God says so. We have got to do it!

It is *so* vital! You might not think it is. Don't be caught off guard when you need it! You have got to have that inside of you. You've got to be built up in the things of God. You've got to weed out all those things that choke out the power and the presence of God in your lives.

Let's pay attention daily. It's so serious — maintain the ground because it is our lives.

Chapter 8
Is This Keeping You From Your Breakthrough?

"My people perish for a lack of knowledge," is what it says in Hosea 4. I think we've seen the "Christian way" done so much that maybe we're missing what the Word of God is actually telling us to do.

Years ago, I started praying the Word of God because I didn't know how to pray and I didn't have a lot of great examples growing up. I knew that if I stuck to the Word, then I wasn't praying wrong. I love to pray the Word. This is something that changes everything for us. When we pray, we expect God to do stuff for us and it's almost like when we're praying, we expect God to send Jesus all over again to die on the cross. We pray as if it's necessary for Him to do that all over again for our prayers to be answered. For example, we constantly say things like, "God please fix this." "God please do this." "God, I need you to_____." That's how I hear so many Christians and I've caught myself praying like that before too!

He has given us all authority on this earth. God is not going to do anything more than He's already done here. Now, He's given over to us the authority to carry on His work and He says, "Greater things shall *you* do." I've studied the Believer's Authority by Kenneth Hagin. In chapter four, on page 29, Brother Hagin wrote that the Lord told him *"You* do something about it!" When I read that passage, it just lifted up in my spirit! We do! We pray as if we're expecting God to come down and do it all over again, and He's already done everything that he needs to do! He's already given us all authority. In Luke 10:19 He says, "Behold! I have given you all authority over every device of the enemy and nothing shall by any means harm you." He has given His authority and His power, *to us*. Even when He called the disciples, He called them and He gave His authority to cast out devils and to lay hands on the sick. He gave us the authority to do it, but we pray as if God's gonna come down and do something about it when, really, He expects *us* to do something about it. He wants *us* to handle it. He wants *us* to bind and loose His Word. Matthew 18:18 says whatever you bind on earth shall be bound in heaven and whatever you loose on earth is loosed in heaven. So, we're sitting here expecting God to bind stuff up for us! We literally pray that way for God to loose us and He says "No, I've given you the authority to bind and to loose. So you do that! *You* are the one!"

Our prayers shouldn't be begging or asking God to come back down and do it. Our prayers should actually come in the form of commanding and demanding what He already purchased for us. We're not making God do anything. He's given us that authority. He expects us to use it. What we're doing is we're demanding, we're commanding the evil forces, the demonic forces. Not once did Christ pray over a sickness. In Acts chapter 3, Peter said to the man at the gate Beautiful, "Rise up and walk." He didn't pray "Oh, that you would be healed. Oh God, that You would heal him." No, Peter used the authority that was given to him, and said "Rise up and walk." God has given us this power and this authority. But unfortunately, because of a "lack of knowledge, my people perish."

This really opened the door for a massive breakthrough in my life because I was at a place where I didn't know how to pray anymore about my situation, and I didn't know what to do. But we go to the Word and the Word teaches us. What it taught me was we don't wrestle against people; we wrestle against principalities. And guess what? Then He tells us He's defeated all of those enemies! He's *already* defeated them! Jesus made an open spectacle of the enemy, he's already defeated! (Colossians 2:15) He's given YOU that authority to bind and loose, and to lay hands on people. He doesn't say pray for sick people. No, what does He say? YOU lay hands on the sick and they shall recover. YOU cast out demons. When you cast out a spirit of infirmity, it has to flee! It has no other choice because you've been given that authority! Too many times, we sit back as Christians, and we're praying, asking God to do something, and He's like, "Man, I gave *you* authority. What are you doing with it?"

Look at the parable of the talents (Matthew 25:14-30). We're gonna stand before God someday. He's given us all of this power, all of this conferred Authority, all of this ability to cast out demons and lay hands on the sick. He's going to say, "What did you do with what I gave you?" My prayer is that He'll say, "Well done." But because of a lack of knowledge, He's gonna look at some people and say, "I never knew you." I don't want that to be the case for me. Seriously, it's His Word that says His people perish for a lack of knowledge. I'm not talking amiss here; this is what His Word says.

Your breakthrough isn't happening because of a lack of knowledge. We need to get in the Word and gain knowledge about what He has to say. He gave me an awesome word picture to go along with this. I'm such a visual person that it helps me to think of things in a word picture. Jesus spoke everything in parables, which are basically word pictures. It would be like you telling your child to go up and clean their room and them sitting on the couch expecting all of the stuff to shift and change and move in their room without doing anything. No, when God tells you to do something, you have to get up and move and do it! You might have to change where you're going or change the atmosphere. You might have to shift some things around. You might have to put some things away forever. You might have to take every thought captive, as it tells us in 2 Corinthians 10:5. It says to take every thought captive and make it obey the Word of God. Listen, we pray, "Oh God, help these thoughts in my head." No! He says "You do it. You take every thought captive!" How many of us get caught up in praying about it, and asking God to do it? He's not coming down to do it for you! He told YOU to take every single thought captive and make it obey the Word of God.

We have interns here at the church. It would be like me saying to one of our interns, "Joni, I want to have a party. I need you to clean up the space and decorate and I'll provide everything. I'll supply everything for this party that you need. I'll provide all the expenses. I want you to invite everybody that will come out, and then I want you to show up and I'll be at this event." It would be like me giving her the directive to do that and then coming back and she's done nothing. She's been sitting there saying to me, "Well, I waited. I waited by the phone. I watched my email for the people to come in, and for you to send them to me." Well nobody ever knew, so they didn't come.

What does the Word of God say? *Go ye! You go!* He says, "You go into all the world and preach the gospel," "You go!" It would be like Joni just sitting there not inviting anybody or I'm telling her to set up and she's not doing any setup.

Here's a real scenario that happened to me: I had somebody coming to clean and I asked them to clean all the floors in my house. Well, I came home and it looked beautiful and then I got to my living room and the carpet was trashed. The grandbabies had been there the day before and there were crumbs and papers all over the carpet. When I asked, she was like, "Oh! I didn't realize you meant that floor, like just the hardwood floors." This is kind of like what we do to God. He asks us to clean up and we omit an area. "I wasn't sure what you were talking about God." How frustrating is that, that we do that to God in these areas where He's given us the authority?

He's given us the charge. *You go. You take every thought captive. You lay hands on the sick. You cast out demons. You bind. You loose.* He's telling us to do it, and we're sitting in our prayer time giving it back to Him to do. "Well, You didn't send anybody into my house." Have you heard that prayer? Maybe you prayed that prayer, "God, send somebody into my house that I can minister to today." Just get up and share Jesus with everybody you encounter! Go, therefore, and preach the gospel, teaching. Make disciples! You make disciples. He's not always gonna send people into your house. Even with our unsaved loved ones, we're like, "Oh God, bring them in!" Really? It's the enemy that blinds the eyes of the unbelievers. What we need to do is use our authority! Listen, this changes everything! It changes the outcome. It changes the result!

If Joni comes back to me and says, "Well, I need you to do that. I don't think I can do that. I don't know how to do that." Or she just doesn't do it (which is mostly what happens), she just doesn't do it at all because, "Well, I wasn't really sure of the directive. I wasn't really sure how

I was gonna do that." It would be like her saying to me, "I'm gonna need you to do that." No, I gave you the charge to go and do this. How frustrating it must be for God as we sit back here and we pray for Him to do it when He's told us to. He gave all authority to the disciples, to anyone that believes. *"These signs shall follow those that believe: In My Name they will cast out demons, they will speak with new tongues, they will take up serpents; and if they drink any deadly thing, it will by no means harm them, they will lay hands on the sick and they will recover."* (Mark 16:17-18)

Those are things that we've been commissioned to do. If you have an unsaved loved one, He says don't even pray for the harvest. He says to pray for laborers because He needs the people that will do it. He says we can command those spirits, so command the spirits that blind their eyes to be removed, that they have to take those blinders off. Then loose the Spirit of Truth upon them. Listen, this changes everything in our time of prayer. So, I have commissioned Joni to do this party. I've told her I'll give her anything that she needs (My God shall supply all of my needs according to His riches in glory, which are unlimited). And Joni is like, she didn't go buy anything because it wasn't her name on the card. I mean, I *authorized* her to do it, but you know, "It wasn't my name on the card. I wasn't sure I could spend that." Absolutely not!

Listen, if you need finances, you don't sit back and pray to God because it's not gonna fall out of the sky and it's not gonna grow on trees! He's given us principles that we follow. If you tithe, Malachi 3 says He'll open the windows of heaven and He'll rebuke the Devourer on your behalf. We have to follow the principles that he put in place. You need to do it! If you want a harvest, you have to sow a seed. If you want something from God, YOU have to do it. YOU make it happen. You can't sit on your couch and be like, "Oh man, I need money. I need finances." Go out and get a job! Work! He'll give you a promotion. And when you do everything as if you're doing it unto the Lord, the promotion will come; the advancement will come. That's how you see things happen.

It talks a lot about laziness in the Word of God. If you don't work, you're not gonna eat. We're sitting back here praying for God to bring in finances and He's given you two hands. He's given you the ability to work. He's giving you a mouth. He's given you things that you can do. He's given you witty ideas and inventions and He keeps putting that in your spirit and you're like, "Oh, I don't know if I can do that. I'm not really sure." He's putting everything in front of you that you need and we sit back and we're praying about it. "I'm praying. I'm praying about that to happen." No, He's telling you to go!

He has given you all authority over everything that the enemy can do. He's asked. He's told us. He's commissioned us to be the ones to go! He's told us that we are to be ready (2 Timothy 4:2). I've commissioned Joni to do this party and go out and invite people in and to have all the supplies and to clean up and to be ready and waiting so that we can have this good time and she's not even ready because she didn't do anything! She was waiting for me, waiting for my approval, waiting for me to show up, waiting for me to come. No, that's not the way you want something to happen when you've commissioned somebody else to do it. This has been such a revelation for me. I feel bad that many times, I've put God in that position. "Like seriously Rhonda, I've given you that authority. I've told you to do that. Why aren't you doing that? Don't sit there begging, asking for Me to do it when I've given you all the power."

The power that raised Christ from the dead dwells in you. That's the power that's inside of you. That's the power we need to be exercising; that we need to be walking in. God has given you authority. Let's be the ones that do something about it. Don't make Him shake His head up there in heaven getting frustrated with us because He's commissioned us to do it and we're sitting here praying and asking Him, "Oh God, I need you to show up! I need you to do something." He's not! He has done everything that He is going to do. He's done everything! Jesus is not coming to do it for you. He doesn't need to! He doesn't need to come back down from the crown to the cross and die again to heal your body! It's already been done. But we pray as if that's the only way we're gonna get healed.

Now His Word says to take communion, *"Do this in remembrance of me"* (Luke 22:19). Acknowledge what's already been done. Stand on what's already been done. It's already been accomplished, it's been done. You go lay hands on the sick. You bind, you loose. You don't fight against people; you fight against principalities. And guess what? It's not even a fight! The only fight is right inside you, and even with that, He's not gonna change your mind for you. You have a free will choice. "Set before you today are life and death." The choice is yours (Deuteronomy 30:19). He's not gonna come in and stop those thoughts. You have a responsibility to take every thought captive and make that thought obey the Word of God. Make your physical body obey the Word of God. Make every demonic force and spirit obey the Word of God. It has no other choice; it has to. He has given you that conferred authority.

Luke 10:17-20 says the seventy returned with joy saying, "Lord even the demons are subject to us in your name." He said to them, "I watched Satan fall from heaven like lightning. You have been given authority over every demon. They are subject to you." Know the devil's not wreaking havoc in your life; you're allowing him to! He has no right! Stand up in your authority today! Stop waiting for God to bind up those spirits. He already did it. The only time He's coming back to do that again is in Revelation. For the time being, He's given you that power and authority; especially over your own domain, over your own body, and over your own life.

Luke 9:1 says Jesus *"called His twelve disciples together and gave them power and authority over all demons, and to cure diseases."* You have the power to heal and authority, in the name of Jesus. You speak the Name of Jesus and those things have to move. They have to shift. Philippians 4:19 says my God shall supply all of my needs. Don't be getting frustrated about finances. Don't be sitting there waiting for those finances. Call those finances forth! If you've sown seed, don't even sit and wait! I call forth the harvest that I've sowed the seed for. Don't sit and wait. You can let it rot in the field while you're sitting and waiting. No, call those things forth. The Word says seedtime and harvest shall not pass away and whatsoever a man sows that shall he also reap (Genesis 8:22 and Galatians 6:7). It's a promise. It's a covenant right that you have, so stop begging! Stop sitting and waiting for God to do something. Get up and start commanding and demanding in the spirit realm every promise, every right that He's given you the power and authority to walk in. This really changes everything.

There are some areas in your life that you haven't gotten a breakthrough in because of a lack of knowledge; because you've been praying amiss. You've been praying and asking God to come back down and show up and He's like, "No, no. Listen, I gave you that authority. I gave you that power. I gave you that right. You open your mouth. You go do this. You take action. You put faith in it." We're the ones that are going to do it. If you don't do something, nothing is going to happen, and that's why your breakthrough hasn't happened. If you don't do what God has commissioned you to do, nothing's going to happen. If you don't go into all the world, you're not going to see people saved and changed. If you don't lay hands on the sick, they're not going to recover. If you don't take every thought captive, those thoughts are gonna take you captive.

If you don't do something, nothing is going to happen. So, Christian, we've got to stop acting this way, and we need to do it like God has commissioned us to do it. I think we've so missed the boat on this. We've so missed it as the church, as the body of Christ, and as sons and daughters. When you give your child a directive to do something, you are not gonna be okay if they sit there and say, "Well I was waiting for you to come up and help me clean the room." "What? I told you to do this two hours ago! Get to doing it! God has told us to do this in His Word. We've had our entire lifetimes. Let's get busy going about and doing the Father's work! The Father's not coming down to do the work. He already did it! You're the ones. We are the ones that are empowered and told to go do it. I don't want to be a disobedient, passive/aggressive son and daughter.

I don't think we do it intentionally, we just simply do it because of a lack of knowledge; because it's what we've seen other people do around us. But that's why we're not getting a breakthrough. That's why things aren't shifting and changing; because we've been given the authority. You're the one that causes things to shift and change. You're the one that has to choose what you are going to make happen or if you're just gonna sit back and let life happen. If you're doing that, nothing's going to change.

Nothing's going to happen. Stand up in the authority that you have been given. God cannot lie. His Word cannot return void. It says lay hands on the sick and they will recover, but we don't do that.

I was behind my husband the other day, following him home and he stopped at this light. There was a young lady on the corner. He rolled down his window and they were chit-chatting and talking and I didn't know what was going on. I'm parked behind him and she reaches her hands in the vehicle and she's talking to him. We drive away and I call and ask, "What were you doing?" He said, "Well, she said she had a bad day so instead of saying, 'Oh I'll pray for you' I grabbed her hands and said, "Let me pray for you." Then he prayed with her right there. And she's like, "There's a car behind you, though, you can't." He said, "It's just my wife. She'll be ok."

Don't just say you're gonna pray for something. That's not what the Word of God says. We've got to start doing the Word of God. We can't be hearers only. We've got to be doers; and you are going to see things change. You're gonna see things shift when you recognize that you've been given the authority. It's so exciting. When the disciples came back, they were excited and they said, "The demons are subject to us." Every device that the enemy has used against you cannot harm you by any means. When you know your authority, he has to go when you say "go." The Word says resist the devil and he will flee (James 4:7). He has no other choice when you apply the Word of God, not do what you've seen done; not do it the way you assume is the way to do it; not take the lazy way of doing it.

"My people perish for a lack of knowledge." (Hosea 4:6) Get knowledge from the Word of God on how to pray. I was

telling you I had gotten to the place where I just didn't know how to pray about my situation. It was the week before fasting and prayer and I thought, *This is awesome! I'm gonna get knowledge on what I need to do about this.* It was so good to go into fasting and prayer. Some things don't move but by prayer and fasting. But you've gotta do it! God's not gonna fast for you. Carla's fast isn't gonna work for me. Mackenzie's fast isn't gonna do anything for me. Jade's giving and tithing and sowing, as exciting as it is for her, isn't gonna do anything for me. You have to do the Word of God. You can shift your atmosphere right now by commanding the spirits that are hindering you to be gone; by commanding them to put back what they took. You know what? I don't even command them to put it back— they have to put it back better than it was when they touched it! They need to get their grimy little fingerprints off it. I don't want to see a trace of it. And they have to; they're subject to you in the Name of Jesus! You have been given all power and all authority. But too many times, we are perishing in areas of our life simply for a lack of knowledge.

I pray today that this will cause a breakthrough in your life and that you'll rise up with the Word of God and go and do it. I pray you'll lay hands on people, bind and loose things, and do all the things the Word tells you to do. Stop praying for the Father to come upstairs and help you clean your room. It's ugly. I would discipline my child if they did that; if I came up two hours later and they were sitting there saying, "I was waiting for you to come up and help me." "What are you talking about? Look at this mess! I'm not cleaning for you. Clean it up. I told you to do it." God's told us to do it so let's stop waiting on Him.

I think we like that scripture too much, though: *"They that wait upon the Lord...*" (Isaiah 40:31). That word "wait" doesn't just mean sit there. It means serving the Lord. So let's get out and serve the Lord. Stop sitting and waiting for Him. You've been given authority. Let's start shifting things. Let's start breaking through those walls that have no right, and that have no place, and that have no authority over you. The spirits too. Anything hindering you, anything blocking you, anything causing a breakdown in your life, you have authority over that! You have power. You have dominion, in the Name of Jesus. Nothing, not one thing, by any means can harm you, so let's get to walking in our authority.

I pray today that this has been knowledge for you. I know these scriptures. You know these scriptures, but I'm praying today that it moves from your head to your heart and builds excitement for you to go and do what God has commanded us to do, rather than waiting on Him.

Chapter 9
Resist the Devil's Suggestions

Resist the devil's suggestions because he is out to steal, kill and destroy 24/7 (John 10:10). He's like a roaring lion. Now, we don't have to be afraid of that, but we do have to be vigilant, and we have to be aware. We are going to have to resist 24/7 also. When we stop resisting, we are unable to move through the fire. For whatever reason, awareness has really dropped. Maybe we paid attention better in the past, but we aren't paying attention like we should be right now to the devil's devices. Our world today has pitted people against each other; friend against friend, and family against family. It's mask or no mask; Covid-worried or Covid-not-worried; vaccine or no vaccine, democrat or republican. There are just so many areas where there's room for the devil's suggestions in your mind. The devil whispers in people's ears, "You can't do this. You're not going to make it. Everything's just going to go south. Everything's just going to crumble. Nothing's going to be okay anymore." He's just whispering his suggestions and we know those aren't the truth.

First of all, God says that we don't have to be worried; that He already overcame the world for us (John 16:33). He says that nothing is impossible for them that believe. (Matthew 17:20). He also says He's going to work everything out for your good and no weapon formed against you will prosper (Romans 8:28, Isaiah 54:17). You do not have to listen to the devil's suggestions. When they come in, you need to resist them. I know we know this, and I know you're thinking, "Oh, that's just elementary." The Word of God says even the elect will be deceived (Matthew 24:24). Even people that you would never imagine are being taken out by the enemy's suggestions like, "Everybody's against you," "Nobody's on your side," "You loved that person, but they don't love you anymore," "You should just stay away from people," "People are mean or dumb," etc. The enemy doesn't just plant suggestions in your mind; he makes sure every emotion necessary to support that suggestion shows up. You're going to feel like those suggestions are absolutely true.

I mean, there are sides now. Sides! How awful is that, that we have chosen sides? As Christians, we've taken sides in so many different areas. This has allowed offense into the church. It's allowed it into Christians' hearts and minds. It's allowed it into the Christians' thoughts. I don't care what side you're on, or what the reasoning is; whether it's related to the pandemic, legislation, or it's demanded by our government — we still have no reason to take sides! No matter what your heart and your motive were starting out; if you've taken sides, then you need to really check your heart! Check it because the Word of God says in 2 Corinthians 10:3-4 that we walk in the flesh but we do not war according to the flesh, for the weapons of our warfare are not carnal but they're mighty through God to the pulling down of strongholds. Then Ephesians 6:12 tells us our fight is not against flesh and blood.

Hear me, this is God. This is His Word speaking. I don't care what you've rationalized it with, what you've labeled it as, what your pretense was, or what your intentions were. If you are fighting, or you find yourself fighting against flesh and blood, you're not fighting the right source! We wrestle not against flesh and blood, but against principalities, against powers, against the rulers of darkness of this world, and against spiritual forces of evil in heavenly places. That is our only fight. Your fight is not with your family member. It's not with your friend. It's not with your co-worker. It's not with another church member. It's not with your pastor. Listen, you wrestle NOT against flesh and blood. It is the enemy of your soul that is trying to take you out. He's trying to get you offended. He's trying to get you to take sides. He's trying to put you on the opposite side from where you were before. He's trying to take you out. And you know what? You can't just ignore that you've had these thoughts and feelings. If you've had actual feelings of hatred and strife toward the body of Christ, your brothers and sisters in Christ, your neighbors, your friends, and your families, you can't just ignore that! If you ignore it, one day, you'll find yourself outside of the blessing of God. We're gonna find ourselves out of the covering of God, out of the favor of God, out of the power of God, and out of the anointing of God. And, we're not even going to realize that's where we are until we've already rooted ourselves there...if we even ever realize it at all!

Once your thoughts and feelings reach that point, you're rooted there. There is a root that has been dug down inside when we don't resist the devil's suggestions. If you haven't resisted, it's turned into a root of negativity inside you. If you're having negative thoughts, they're not from God. They are NOT from God. Nothing is impossible with God. Everything good comes from God and He tells us to think on these things: whatsoever things are of lovely, are of good report, and are praiseworthy (Philippians 4:8). Those are the things we're going to think on. Any sort of negativity that you have accepted, that you have justified, and that you have rationalized, has turned into a root and you've got to do something about it.

First, you've got to take responsibility for it. "God, I am so sorry that I allowed this to go to this place. I know what Your Word says. Your Word says I have no fight with another human being. They are my brothers and sisters and I am called to love with God's unconditional love. Any negativity, hatred, strife that is built up inside of me is sin and it is wrong." It *is* sin and it *is* wrong. Listen to me: it will take you out of the blessing of God! It's going to take you out of the anointing. It's going to take you out of the power of God. It's going to take you out of the presence of God and you're not even recognizing it. You don't even realize it! You don't even know that you're being taken out of the presence and the power of God right now. It's so vital and so important for us to pay attention to this. We've got to uproot it right now in order to get ourselves connected back to the vine. You've severed yourself from the vine if you've dwelt in that negative place; that place of hatred, that place of strife, that place of gossip and busy bodying. It's not of God and it's damaging you.

The suggestions of the devil that have come into your mind are sinful. It doesn't matter the reason, whether they're justified, or whether you've just rationalized them. They are not of God. We have to wake up and realize what has happened here. The enemy is causing division inside of your heart and mind. He is taking you out and he is going to weaken you and you aren't even going to know it or realize it. We've got to catch this!

Now maybe there's already a root inside of you. You're gonna have to dig that root out, sever it, cut it off, and resist the devil. James 4:7 says resist the devil and he will flee from you. Once that root is in there, you're gonna have to really dig and dig and dig and push with that shovel. You're gonna have to resist, and resist, and resist; especially where you've allowed, embraced, and accepted this negativity, this hatred, this strife, this division, this taking of sides which is not of the Kingdom of God.

Behold the commanded blessing is where there is unity (Psalm 133:1-3). I don't want to walk in any other place; especially right now with everything going crazy in the world. If you're outside of the umbrella of God, you're crazy! Get back under the umbrella of God. Get in unity with your brothers and sisters! Get on your face and repent before God for being out of unity with the family of God and your brothers and sisters in Christ. Get back under the blessing and covering of God. It is so important that we get to the root of this. We have to dig this root out and deal with it because we're going to find ourselves in a place we don't want to be. We can't afford to be in that place. I cannot afford to be offended.

You also cannot afford to be offended. We have got to be able to walk in the supernatural. We've got to be able to declare a thing and it will be. We've got to be able to speak and it shall come forth. You have to make sure you remain unoffendable. I feel like so many have embraced negativity and offense. The Word of God says even the elect will be deceived. So many have embraced it under the guise of, "It's okay because this is what we have to do. We have to take sides. We have to tear one another down. We have to speak against them. We have to allow this inside our hearts. We have to tell everybody we know all this negativity that the devil's suggesting in our minds."

No, you do not! Cover your mouth! Bite your tongue! The Word of God says if you don't have anything good to say, don't say anything. That's not your mama's old adage, that's the Word of God. Ephesians 4:29 says let no corrupt communication proceed out of your mouth, only that which builds, encourages, and edifies. If it's not building, if it's not encouraging, and if it's not edifying, it's not God. If it is not God, it is poisoning you. It is tainting you. Don't be deceived. Whatever a man sows that is what they are going to reap (Galatians 6:7).

So, shake yourself out of this! Shake yourself out! Get on your face before God and just repent before Him and guess what? He says He's going to come in and He's going to heal your land! (2 Chronicles 7:14) He's going to restore you. You can change everything right now just by resisting those suggestions that the enemy is putting in your mind. It could be suggestions of negativity towards other people, but it also could be suggestions of negativity toward yourself. For instance, the devil might be telling you, "You just can't do this," "You're just not cut out for this," "You're just tired," or "You're just weary." There are so many scriptures in the Word of God that promise He'll take your heavy burdens and if you are weary, He's gonna give you rest. He is a good and faithful God, but we have got to resist the devil! We can't allow his suggestions.

He's planting those suggestions in your mind. 24/7 he's coming at you. You've got to be aware of the enemy's advances and his devices. Don't let pride keep you from repenting and humbling yourself before God. Don't let pride keep you out. Pride is going to come before a fall. So, if in any way you hear the Word of the Lord that's been spoken and you're like, "Oh, maybe I've done that," "Oh I've definitely been guilty of that," "Oh yeah, I've got some strife," or "I've got some negative things to say," please repent. Maybe that's you right now. You need to repent before the Lord and humble yourself and pray and then He's gonna restore your land! You cannot afford to be offended. You cannot afford to sacrifice the anointing, the power, and the presence of God, and that is *exactly* what you're doing! Do not be deceived!

I have seen so many people pick one scripture out of the entire Bible and try to stand on that one scripture. Listen to me – the Word of God says over and over to watch your thoughts, to watch your words, to think on these things, to speak these things, let no corrupt communication come out of your mouth, etc. It says it over and over again. If those things are going on in your heart and mind, you are NOT following God. It is a dangerous place to be. You have fallen for the suggestions of the enemy and that is not a place you want to remain in. There is probably even a root that is already locked in and anchored you into this. Cut that root right out! Swallow any kind of pride, and just come back before God and get yourself free of that! Get yourself free and think about things that are good, think about things that are lovely, speak true things that are praiseworthy things, and that are good. And resist, resist, resist, over and over again, the devil's suggestions. Then he will have to flee from you! Heed the Word of the Lord. Uproot that thing and get yourself under the safety of the blessing and favor of the Lord as quickly as you possibly can. Don't delay.

Chapter 10
I Know It

How many of us know a know-it-all? They know everything! You start talking and their response is, "I know it." Teenagers? You start explaining something to them and they say, "I know it." No, they don't know it. They haven't lived on the earth as long as you have. I mean, "They don't know it, but I know it!"

How about a 4-year-old in a phase when the child thinks they know everything? For real! They say it as fact. "I know it. I know it." "No, you don't even know what two plus two is." They know! Oh yes, they do. According to them, they know it.

I want to talk to you about "I know it" because I caught myself saying "I know it" regarding the things of God and His Word because, you know, I've heard it. It's been read. I play it. I read it. I go to church services, Bible studies, classes, all of those things. You know, we can tend to stop doing those things because we think, "I already know it." You know when I really caught myself? It was on my Bible app and I was reading the daily verse. I love the portion where it has related scriptures to your last highlight. If you didn't know that, on the homepage, there are a bunch of verses related to whatever scripture you last highlighted. I would begin to read, "For God so loved the world blah blah blah blah blah blah blah," and not continue to read because I know what it says. Right? How many of us have found ourselves doing that? If I know the verse, I don't even continue to read it because "I know it."

Well, scripture is just like oxygen. You take in oxygen and you exhale oxygen and then you take in oxygen again. Does it ever get boring or old or unnecessary for you to take in oxygen again? No! The Word of God is literally just like oxygen. It says it is living, it is alive, it is quickening, and it is powerful. So every time you take it in, you could literally read the same verse every single day of your life, and every day it will be fresh to you. The Word of God is like fresh oxygen to you. Jesus calls it your daily bread. Whatever you need, this is your daily bread. It's fresh and new every single day. I've trained myself (now that God put his finger on this) to finish that scripture even if "I know that." If you know it so well, you'd better quote it out loud and then finish it without looking at it. But finish reading that scripture because the "I know it" can actually stop you from getting the oxygen you need!

"I know it" stops us from coming to classes. We have a character class that is taught at our church. We think, "I know everything there is to know about character" or "Oh you know what? I've got great character. I don't need to go to that class. I know it." We never ever should get to the place where we feel like we know it all. Actually, God warns us in the scripture of getting to that place. It's very dangerous, lest you fall into sin. Every time there's a class offered, I still go and attend the classes. I sit and listen. You know what I showed up at 7:30 church service even though I wasn't preaching. My daughter-in-law, Mindy was preaching. I wanted to sit under the Word of God, fresh and new, every single day. We can never allow it to get old in our minds. It is our oxygen. It is our life. It is fresh daily bread every time you read it. Every time you read it, it will bring a breakthrough. Every time you read it, it will go forth and perform what it is sent to do.

But we've got to not be like, "I know it" because then we're not reading it. It's keeping us from being a hearer of the Word and faith comes by hearing the Word of God. Notice it doesn't use the word, *heard*. Does it say faith came by what you heard yesterday, in last week's class, or last Sunday? Faith comes by what you heard? No, that's not what it says. Faith comes by *hearing* (Romans 10:17). That is current. That is fresh and new. If you need faith, you need the Word of God fresh and new. I remember one of the times in this past year when I was in the ER. I had gotten a devastating report. Another death sentence. I listen to the healing scriptures at least twice a day. I hear them all the time. I'm listening to them faithfully and what happened when I got that news? My initial response was, "Well, I listen to it all the time. I have the Word in my spirit, like, I know that. I know what it says." But I started to panic. And then I was like, "Wait a minute. I'm going to open my Word. I'm going to open my Word and I'm going to play the scriptures so I can hear them and read along with them also. The scripture that stood out in that moment, which again, I thought, I know this I've heard it probably a gazillion times (I mean literally with how much I listened to it), was 2 Corinthians 1:10. It says, "*I have delivered you from death, I am delivering you, and if you will trust me, I will yet deliver you.*" It was the exact Word. It was fresh and alive and like oxygen. It was new for me. In that moment, it was exactly what I needed to hear. It was my daily bread.

But I could have been kept from that Word that I needed to hear by thinking, "I know it." I'm so faithful to put the Word of God in me, so the "I know it" could have kept me from hearing it at the moment I really needed it. It could have kept me from the very healing that I needed. So many times the "I know it" keeps us from applying it to our lives. I was counseling with someone and they're like, "I'm in my Bible like I've never been before. I'm reading it every single day. But how do I keep ending up in this place? I keep ending up in this place of frustration and offense, even though I'm reading the Word of God." Here's the next level of "I know it": We have to act on what we hear! James 1:22 says, "*Don't just listen to God's Word. You must do what it says!*" This isn't me saying this; this is the Word of God! This is a command. And yeah, I'm talking to you *mature* Christians, because the "I know it" sometimes keeps us from "I need to do it. I need to act on it because we keep from even being hearers of it.

I think sometimes we get comfortable with the "I know it," and with saying, "Amen. That sounds good!" We get comfortable with that and it stops us from actually doing what we need to be doing. Let's finish what it says. This is how the verse ends - ...*otherwise, you're fooling yourself.* How many times have you thought, *God, I just don't understand why this isn't happening. Why aren't you coming through right here?* Because, if we aren't doing what it says, we're fooling ourselves! "*If you listen to the Word and don't obey it's like glancing at your face in a mirror, but if you look carefully into the perfect law that sets you free...*" That's the key. *If.*

We come into church Sunday after Sunday hearing the Word of God. We need to become quick, obedient children of the Word of God! Quick and obedient! I read a scripture and it wasn't even a command at all. It was saying there are blessings for people that take care of the poor and consider them (Psalm 41:1). I immediately put down my Bible, got to my phone, and sponsored a Compassion

International child I had just heard about in church that week but I hadn't done anything with it yet. We need to *quickly* obey the Word of God. Whatever God puts His finger on in your life, when He puts His finger on it, just say, "Yes, Lord. Okay, I'm gonna do it." Then promptly go and do it! That's the kind of response we're supposed to have to everything we hear from the Word of God.

"Amen" is not good enough. "Amen" will keep you deceived. "Amen" will keep you in bondage. "Amen" will keep you broken. Action is what will break through. When we act on the Word of God, it will break through anything and everything we are facing. There is nothing more powerful. But we've got to act on the Word of God!

It's like this. I have a gift, and it is the Word of God all wrapped up in a beautiful gift bag. In it is everything that my daughter-in-law Mindy is going to need for life. Anything and everything. This is a *gift*, this is the Word of God. This is what we're all given. I present the gift to her, and imagine this is what happens:

Mindy: "Thank you."
Me: "But, aren't you going to open it?
Mindy: "I know what's in it."
Me: "But you need to open it.   "
Mindy: "I already know what it is."
Me: "But you won't open it?"
Mindy: "I mean, I know what's in here. You gave me the same thing yesterday."

That's what we do with the precious treasure and gift that God has given us. We say, "Thank you so much," we receive it, we hear it, we accept it, and we even know what it contains. But are we acting on it?

The laws of God produce such incredible power and promises, but we have to act on them. We have to obey God in those things. Then He will do incredible and powerful things. Luke 6:46 says, "Why do you call me Lord, Lord and not do what I tell you?" OUCH. This is the Word of God. 1 John 3:18 says, *"Let us not love in word or talk but in deed and truth."* You say "Everybody loves God, right? I love God." No, the Word of God says, *"'If you love me you'll obey me. If you love me keep my commandments.'"* So we're not showing love and we're not showing faith unless we are acting on the Word of God. We could easily say, "I know it" and that makes us think we are doing it already. Are we though? Are we? When God brings a fresh Word to us through a Sunday service, through a sermon we're listening to, through a podcast, in a class, in our group, or when we're hearing something from the Word of God, are we acting on it? Are we *quickly* acting on it? James 2:17 says, *"Faith by itself, if it does not have works, is dead."*

Some of you are believing big! You've got faith. You've heard the Word and nothing's happening because the Word of God says faith without doing is *nothing*. It's nothing. That's why you see so many powerless Christians; so many powerless *mature Christians.*

Titus 1:16 gets rough. I mean, sometimes the Word of God is brutal. But, you know what? Sometimes it has to be. Clearly, we're not moving if we're coddled. God knows what He's doing. He knows He's got to be blunt with us. Titus 1:16 says, *"Such people claim they know God but they deny him by the way they live."* I don't even want to read the rest of this verse, but this *is* The Bible. I'm sorry, this is not me saying it. I'm serious, I was under such conviction. I still am when I'm writing this. It's a good conviction. It's awesome and it's an exciting conviction because when we choose to obey, it opens up new levels of power in our lives. I need the power of God! I don't want to walk a day or a moment in this life and in this world without the power of God residing in me. It's like when Moses said, "I will not go anywhere without your presence, God." We need to be like that, "I'm not going to go anywhere without your presence, God."

Titus 1:16 goes on to say *"These are detestable, disobedient, worthless for doing anything good."* God help us! When I skip over those verses, when I just say "Amen," "I know it," and I leave and I continue in the same mindset and I continue doing the same things, it's *worthless.* I can't live in that place. I can't afford to live in that place. I literally can't afford to live in that place. I don't know, maybe you're comfortable outside of the power of God. I am *not* comfortable outside of the power of God. I need the power of God for every breath that I take in my lungs, literally.

It's found in John 14:15, by the way, *"If you love me, keep my commandments."* James 4:17 goes on to say, *"If anyone then knows the good they ought to do, and don't do it, it's sin."* We like to think of sin as all those big things. It's when we hear the Word of God and the Holy Spirit speaks to our hearts, and we don't do it, that's sin. This is actually exciting because you are the remnant of God and He is cleansing His house to make it without spot or wrinkle. So, when I get the conviction of God, it doesn't make me think, *Oh God, I'm a horrible wretch.* No, it makes me excited! It makes me say, "I am powerful." It gets me excited because when we do it, we can have confidence that He will perform His Word.

Hebrews 4:12 was speaking of the church. *"For indeed the gospel the good news was preached to all of them as well as us."* We're all hearing this same thing today, and every week you hear the Word of God at church. *"But the word which they heard did not profit them."* Well, why didn't it profit them? *Because it was not being mixed with faith in those who heard it.* Faith, as we have heard, is action. It's not agreement. It's not "Amen." It's not, "Oh, that's good Pastor. Go on. Keep going, Pastor." No. Faith is action! If we don't combine the Word we hear with action, it profits us nothing. That's how you can sit in the same congregation with some people prospering, having breakthroughs, and having victory, and others not.

If you're not experiencing victory right now, I'm not condemning you because God spoke this Word to *me* so that He can make more power available to me. So you take it for yourself! Don't worry about anybody else. This is not judgment. This is not condemnation. If we hear the Word, and we do it, unlimited, surpassing power is available to us. We will walk through anything and everything! I pray that my life has been such that anything and everything that I've walked through, you can see me walking through with peace, joy, confidence, faith, and love. I don't want to walk any other way because I need to walk in obedience to the Word of God. There's no profit to just hearing the Word of God and not doing it.

Do you know that even the devil knows the Word of God? That's kind of scary. The devil tempted Jesus (Luke 4:1-12). Doesn't it say he knows the Word of God? In James 2:19 it says that even the demons know and tremble. That's scary!

So, that "I know it. I know it all" place is true even with the demons! They know it, too! "I know it" doesn't make any of the promises and power of God available to you just because you know it! Even demons "know it." We actually have to DO the Word of God!

I love this one – John 5:8-9. It's so funny to me; it's amusing. There was a paralyzed man who *could not walk.*

He was paralyzed. He was laying down, and he could not move. There was no way.

Jesus came up to him and said, "Rise up and walk!"

"But I'm paralyzed! Don't you see me, God? Like what are you saying?" How many of us are in that place? "But God, can't you see my situation? Don't you see what's going on? This is really real! I can't." This man literally could not walk!

But Jesus said, "Get up and walk," and guess what? HE DID! He did it! He put action to it! What was impossible, at the Word of God and in obedience to the Word, *became possible!*

Whatever your situation is, whatever it is that you're going through, *obey* the Word of God. Do it and watch the impossible happen for you, too! When you do it, God performs miracles!

I just crack up at it every time. Can you imagine this man lying there UNABLE to move? I mean, I *can* imagine the thoughts because I'm human, too! I get your situations and the things you're going through, and Jesus just says, "Hey, get up and walk! Get up! Get up!"

Whatever situation you're in, get up! Get up and walk! Don't just lay there! Don't make excuses. Don't be like, "But God, this spouse you gave me…" "But God, this body you gave me…" "But God, this place you put me in…" I live in New York State. I've heard people say, "I hate New York." We need to get out of that! I don't care where I live! It doesn't matter what state you live in. We live in the Kingdom, so every day, I walk in blessing! Every day, I walk in victory! The government doesn't dictate what I get to walk in; the Word of God does! You can make all the excuses in the world; it all boils down to nothing but our obedience to the Word of God. It all boils down to that because the Word is living and active!

Let's read all of Hebrews 4:12, and you know what? It's crazy because when you start reading it your brain goes, "blah, blah, blah, blah, blah" because *you know it!* You've heard me say this verse a thousand times. *Never* shut your ear off to the Word of God! *"For the word of God is living and powerful, and sharper than any two-edged sword, piercing even to the division of soul and spirit, and of joints and marrow, and is a discerner of the thoughts and intents of the heart."* When the Word is being performed and spoken it's doing surgery God's putting his finger on things in your life. He's speaking to your spirit. He's saying "Don't do this" and "I want you to do this." You've already thought of things while you're reading that God is speaking to you. "Oh I need to do that," "I need to stop that," "I need to go there," "I need to not go there."

Action is required. The promises of God are not automatic, and they are not for everyone. They are *available* for everyone, but they are not *for* everyone. They are only for those who hear and do and put action to the Word of God. It has to be continued action, all the way through. It's not a one-time action. I pray that you never think that you get to such a place of "maturity" that you "know it." I never want to get to that place. I always want to be open to hearing the Word of God. I always want to attend classes. I always want to sit under teaching. I always want to hear the Word of God, fresh and new, and take advantage of any opportunity that I can. I'm hungry for the Word of God. I never want to put myself in the position where I know too much, where I've learned it all. It's such a dangerous place to be. That's why mature Christians fall away. It's sad because "I know it" will actually cause you to fall away.

Sometimes our knowing is skewed and misinterpreted and even taught wrong. Take the Christmas story for example. I know many of you thought that the wise men were at the nativity and they weren't. You could have wrong teaching about something. You can have a wrong gut theology based on an experience you had from the Word of God. That's now in the "I know it" zone. And like that 4-year-old kid that doesn't actually "know it," your knowing it is wrong. It is amiss. It's not actually the truth from the Word of God at all.

We need to take the Word of God fresh and new, and we need to put action to it because Hebrews 4:2 tells us that without action it's not going to profit us anything. Here's an action verse. I'm not going to judge, I'll let you judge yourself. If you've put action to this, there will be results from it. Matthew 6:33 says "*'But seek first the Kingdom of God.'*" That's a command. We have to put action to it. Are you seeking first the Kingdom of God above everything else in your week or in your day? It's not profiting you if you're not obeying it. The promise with this is "*'Seek first the kingdom of God and His righteousness, and then all these things will be added unto you.'*" But we don't do it because "we know it." The gospel's been so saturated. All Christians just "know." We know what it says. We've already heard it. We say things like, "I don't need to make any effort in my day to seek God or go to His house. You know I already know it."

Pastors, *hear me.* Your "I know it" could be keeping you powerless, worthless, and unfruitful. It's His Word. I pray,

"God, keep me from ever getting to that place." We need to act on the Word of God immediately and obey it.

Here are some action items from the Word of God:

Forgive and Forgive Quickly

If you have any unforgiveness in your heart right now, I'm commissioning you from the Word of God. In Matthew 6 it says forgive as I have forgiven you. He forgave us when we were still sinners.

So, when stuff is still going wrong, and that person's still not acting the way that they should, we forgive. Forgiveness isn't for them; forgiveness is for us because it's obeying the Word of God. It makes the power of God available to us, and it keeps offense and bitterness from our lives. So forgive those past things. What about the things that are going to come up tomorrow? Let's not even wait till tomorrow! It's probably going to happen before you leave the house. You might already have to forgive me because you're upset with what I wrote.   These aren't just things we say because they sound good. They are things you actually have to do and that you need to do for the power of God to be unleashed in your life. Forgive quickly. Hold no record of wrongs. First Corinthians 13:5 tells us that.

Now listen husbands and wives, if your spouse does it, don't you go throwing the Word of God at them. Don't hold it over them that they're not supposed to hold any record of wrong. Mind your own business and deal with yourself! If everybody deals with themselves, then nobody has any problems. Deal with yourself. *You* hold no record of wrong. When that thing comes up (because the enemy's *going* to bring it up in your head; all the things they've already done to you), you have to let it go. Refuse him and say, "No. I hold no record of wrongs. I forgive."

Do Good to Those Who Haven't Been Good to You

No, don't just keep your mouth shut. Don't just pray for them in your home. Nope. The Bible says to *do good to them* (Matthew 5:44).

My husband actually preached a sermon on this. He encouraged us to anonymously send a blessing to someone who did us wrong and also to send blessings to encourage people who hadn't wronged us. I obeyed and I obeyed quickly.

I sent my anonymous blessings and I sent my blessings for people that I wanted to encourage so nobody knew if I was saying I'm sorry or if I was saying I love you, but we're actually supposed to do something good for that person. It is so freeing. It is so liberating for you. It keeps you from bondage. It keeps you from having your power taken from you. It keeps you from being outside of the blessing and favor of God. We've got to obey quickly and be free of offense.

Trust God with All Your Heart and Lean Not on Your Own Understanding

That means when His Word says it, we do it. We don't lean on our own understanding or our own rationalizations. We just trust God. Whatever that thing is you have going on, just say it out loud to God, "I trust You." When fear starts coming up, say, "No. I trust God." When the devil starts lying to you, say, "No. I trust God." It's not something you just do once.

I've found that taking action and obeying the Word of God is necessary every second of every day. It's not something that we can sit here right now and say, "Yep, I'm going to put action to that." No, it's you doing it 50 times this week. It might be more, it might be less.

Love Unconditionally

Love the least of these. The ones that you consider the least important? Those are the ones we love. This is the Word of God (Matthew 25, 1 Corinthians 13, 1 Peter 4:8).

Tithe

The Word of God says in Matthew 23:23, *"You tithe, this you ought to do."* Don't be mad at me. Your obedience is your life. My obedience, thank God, is my life, because I'm gonna jump! I'm gonna obey quickly. Be a cheerful giver, and consider the poor.

Go Into All the World

Go into all the world, and it says if you can't go, then send someone. So go or send. Make sure the gospel is being spread. That's a command for everybody; it's not just to preachers. That's for you. That's in your workplace, in your home, in your family, and in your circle of influence. You're to take the goodness of God everywhere you go. Talk about how awesome God is. Talk about how good He is. Go and do! Go into your world.

Don't just go and show up for work Monday morning. No, you have Jesus. You have this gift. You have everything that people need. You have the answer. Jesus is the answer for every single person. He's the answer for the poor, and He's the answer for the executive, the business owner, and

Don't just go and show up for work Monday morning. No, you have Jesus. You have this gift. You have everything that people need. You have the answer. Jesus is the answer for every single person. He's the answer for the poor, and He's the answer for the executive, the business owner, and the elite. He's the answer. Everything that people need, you have! He tells us to go with that. So if we're not opening our mouths and sharing about the goodness of God, I'm sorry to tell you, it's disobedience and the Word isn't going to profit us.

Praise God in All Situations

You've just got to crank up the praise music sometimes. Our church did a 21 Days of Praise celebration. You can do this on your own. Just commit to doing 21 days of praise. I would encourage you not to just praise when you're at church. Will you praise with me 24/7? I've even been putting it on at night when I'm sleeping. I have to put it down low because even when I wake up in the middle of the night my foot's moving because when I say praise music, I mean shouting clamorously and foolishly praising God! I mean getting radical before God, and making all those other things go dim.

Let's put action behind our hearing. We don't get to live any way we want and expect God to show up powerfully. You don't get to just do that. You don't get to say, "I want *this* harvest." You have to pick the seed. It's only what you plant that you harvest. Literally, you can't pick the harvest. You have seed and what you choose to plant is what you're going to live in. Oh please…today, if you're hearing me, put action to it! Don't be overwhelmed with all the things. God's gonna work on individual things in you. It's not like you have to go out tomorrow and wear a halo and be perfect. I mean, maybe you are. I'm definitely not perfect (and my husband said, "Amen!"). Clearly, I'm not perfect because I'm teaching you this message from what God has spoken to me. He's always working on something in us and that's awesome. That's good! I love getting one thing conquered then I'm like, "All right God, bring on the next thing. Let's go. Let's go!" He brings you deeper and deeper in the things of Him with more confidence and more power available to you.

It's time to change forward. Change is an action word. Change forward is the direction of our action. We're gonna choose to change forward. We're not changing backward, we're not changing the same, we're changing forward, and we're gonna put action to the Word of God. Then we're going to watch the Word be powerful and active in our lives like never before. As we put more action to the Word, we are going to see the harvest come in like crazy. The world needs to see the power of God in you. Every single person in the world needs to see the power of God in every single one of us. Your world needs to see the power of God. Your home needs to see the power of God, and the only way to do it is to put action to it. When we choose today to quickly obey – to *quickly* obey His Word – we know, we know, *we know* that He backs up His Word. He watches over His Word and He will perform His Word.

So God, today we combine our hearing and faith with action. Thank you, Jesus. Even right now, you're doing a thing. You're doing work, Jesus. Thank you, thank you, thank you, Jesus.

You can't afford to say "I know it" or to be hearers only. Let's put action to it!

Chapter 11
Trust Beyond Your Own Understanding

This is so important because we have such a natural need to try and understand. Sometimes it's a major challenge because we try to understand and figure everything out. We try to make things make sense to us. But that's actually not faith. We're not trusting beyond our own understanding if it's stuff that we can figure out and we can attain. That's just not even faith at all. That's not trusting in God's ways. His ways are higher than our ways, and His thoughts are higher than our thoughts (Isaiah 55:9). We can't expect to understand everything that's going on around us, but we must trust beyond our own understanding and that's a learning process. That's a daily process. That's something you have to continually do. Whenever things come up, you have to trust beyond your own understanding.

It's tempting to be limited to only what we can grasp, see in front of us, and understand. I love the scripture passage (I love all the scripture passages) Proverbs 3:5-6 in the Amplified Classic version. Verse 5 says *"Lean on, trust in, and be confident in the Lord with all of your heart and mind and do not rely on your own insight or understanding."* It's simply the Word of God. It's what He tells us to do; to not lean on our own insight and our own understanding. It's difficult. I get it. It's a lot harder than it sounds. Verse 6 says, "In all your ways know, recognize, and acknowledge Him, and He will direct and make straight and plain your paths." Wow, that one scripture right there! If we could just apply that one scripture to everything that we face, everything that we encounter, and every portion of our day.

Trust in God. Trust in and be confident in the Lord, not in our own understanding, and not in our own insight. Trusting. Being confident in the Lord and in His ways even when it makes no rational sense. It's nonsense to our human mind, but God is *super*natural. He is not limited to our insight and our understanding. But, when we try to make His thinking fit ours, we're limiting Him to our own insight and understanding. That's why He tells us to lean on Him, trust in Him, and be confident in Him and in His ways. We have got to train our minds to do that.

This is not an easy topic. I understand. I am human, just like you. We all have to walk in this and practice it. We need to learn how to trust in, lean on, and be confident in the Lord; not to rely on our own insight and understanding. The Word of God tells us in Matthew 18: 3-5 AMP, "*'Truly I say to you, unless you repent (change, turnabout) and become like little children [trusting lowly, loving, forgiving] you can never enter the kingdom of heaven [at all].'*" It's saying right there that we can't even enter the supernatural realm unless we become like children. They just trust! They don't have to figure everything out. They just simply trust. God is telling us in His word that we've got to be like those little children in that trust level. It goes on to say whoever will humble themselves and become like this little child [trusting, lowly, loving, and forgiving] is the greatest in the Kingdom of Heaven. If you want to see greatness in the Kingdom of Heaven, we've got to trust Him and be confident in the Lord. We don't need to try to figure everything out or lean on our own insight and our own understanding. It is so awesome! He's given us His Word. It gives us everything that we need to live this kingdom life; this supernatural life.

You cannot fit the supernatural into our own finite, limited insight and understanding. Yet, we try to do that all the time. I just want this to get so deep inside your spirit – trust beyond your own understanding. When you're in the middle of something that's hard, I want you to remind yourself of this. I want you to hear my voice telling you, "Trust beyond your own insight and understanding." Trust beyond it, because beyond it is where the supernatural is. If we stay within our own insight and our own understanding, we cannot even enter into the Kingdom of heaven (Matthew 18:3-5). We need to trust beyond our own understanding. I remind myself of that. Sometimes we have to coach ourselves. Sometimes we have to encourage ourselves. You've got to trust beyond your own understanding.

In that passage we just read in Matthew 18:3-5, it says we can't even begin to enter the Kingdom of Heaven unless we trust like a little child with childlike faith and trust. You know what? That's hard sometimes! When we've gone through life and we're grown, and we have these experiences, and we've seen things, and we try to understand, and we try to rationalize, and we try to use our own insight. It's so hard when we've lived any amount of life. Children have that childlike faith because they don't have experiences that speak differently; that speak doubt and unbelief to them. The next scripture that I have for you is 2 Corinthians 5:7. This is the Word of God that says *"For we walk by faith [we regulate our lives and conduct ourselves by our conviction or belief respecting man's relationship to God and divine things, with trust and holy fervor; thus we walk] not by sight or appearance."* The New King James Version says *"We walk by faith and not by sight."* The amplified breaks it down to say we need to trust with holy fervor. You've got to hold on to that trust because it's so easy for our own insight and our own understanding to come in and try to rationalize and try to reason with what's going on. When we're doing that, it's so limiting that we can't even enter the supernatural. We're cutting off the supernatural the moment we try to rationalize it in our own understanding.

When we're walking by what we can see, we are not walking in faith. Walk by faith, not by sight; not by what you can see, not by what you can understand, not by what you can rationalize. We need to walk by that childlike faith that causes us to be able to enter into the supernatural realm. It just makes me giddy like a child to even think of the supernatural. I love the supernatural so much. I don't want to be limited to my own understanding of this natural realm. Maybe some of you have been discouraged because that's what you've been limited to. You've been focused on what you can see. You've been walking by what you can see in your experiences. It's tempting for all of us to try to understand and figure it out, but that's not God's will for us. That's such a discouraging place because the supernatural can't even prevail in that place. We want to walk in the supernatural. I love seeing stuff that is impossible. I love the God of the impossible, our miracle-working God. When we trust with that childlike faith, that's when we get to walk in that. That's when we get to walk in the Kingdom. The supernatural will start happening when we walk by faith and not by our own insight and understanding.

When something happens to us, it's so easy for us to base the next thing on that discouragement or the thing that didn't work out. We couldn't understand it, and we can't make sense of it, and we don't know why. I am telling you, trust beyond that place! Go beyond! Trust with childlike faith. Get excited and giddy about the supernatural and being able to prevail in that circumstance. Then you won't be left discouraged, confused, disappointed, and trying to wrap your head around what's going on. Listen, you don't have to understand! I love that so much.

God showed me a depiction years and years ago and it's helped me so much in this understanding. It was one single piece of a puzzle. If I had one single piece of the puzzle, that's like my life in comparison to eternity. Even just in my own life, we've got eternity, and we've got the worldwide eternity, so it's such a big picture that God sees. God sees that whole puzzle. He sees the whole thing. But if I have one tiny piece that represents my life throughout all eternity, I would never know what that whole puzzle looks like, no matter how long I contemplate on that piece to try to get insight. If I had one single piece of a puzzle, it is impossible to figure out what that whole puzzle is.

When God revealed that to me, it made it so much easier for me to just trust and say, "God, I know I don't see the big picture. I know I don't see it how You see it. I don't think the way You think. I know I only see a little tiny piece of this whole thing. So, I'm gonna trust that You're a Supernatural Guy. I'm gonna trust that You know my end from the beginning. You aren't gonna quit on me. I'm gonna trust that you work all things out for my good even when I don't understand, even when I can't wrap my brain around it; *especially* when I can't." That's when the supernatural kicks in. It brings it to the Kingdom level where God can show up on the scene and be present. There's actually a scripture about this and it's found in 1 Peter 5:7. "Casting the whole of your care [all your anxieties, all your worries, all your concerns, once and for all] on Him, for He cares for you affectionately and cares about you watchfully."

He cares deeply for us. He cares so deeply for you that He will make a way where there seems to be none. And you know what? It's so much more fun when it's supernatural! It's so much more fun when God comes in and does what is not even possible. It confounds people. It's beyond our understanding. God will do abundantly above all you can ask, think, or even imagine (Ephesians 3:20). He goes beyond your insight and understanding. He's not limited to it, so let's join Him in that. Let's go beyond our own limited understanding and insight, and trust beyond that place. Let's become like little children.

This doesn't mean becoming unintelligent. It's not that. It's not like you check your brain at the door. But you do have to trust beyond your own understanding. It's actually spiritually intellectual to believe that God is so vast and He thinks beyond what the smartest brain on the face of the earth can fathom. It's actually enlarging our intellect to believe that God can go beyond our limited thinking. Even at my best thinking, God goes beyond that. He goes beyond my understanding and my finite thinking. He is an infinite God. He is able to do abundantly above. His power is surpassing. It's not even on a human level. When we try to humanize our God with our understanding and our insight, that is cutting off the Kingdom. It's cutting off the supernatural from our lives. So, if you've been discouraged in any area, I want you to jump into that childlike faith and get giddy about the fact that God's gonna do something super crazy beyond your understanding, beyond your insight, beyond what you can even imagine. If you stretch your imagination as far as you possibly can, God still can go beyond that. So we walk by that kind of faith; not by what we can see and feel. We become like little children and we trust and lean on God in all confidence, beyond our own understanding.

I hope this has been encouraging and helpful to you. Just stay out of that place where you have to control and figure it all out for yourself. Avoid thinking you've got to understand and you've just got to know. You are *never* gonna know how the mind of God works; that intricate, that infinite, that all-powerful mind. You are not God. When we're trying to think with our limited human minds, we are always going to fall short. I pray today that you will gain a childlike faith and trust that says, *I don't understand everything. I don't have all knowledge. I am NOT God and infinite in my wisdom. He knows everything about everything.*

If somebody just spent their entire lifetime gaining knowledge, they'll still never gain all the knowledge that God has. He knows the solution. He knows what you should do. He knows His power. We need to get on board with that. Let's get childlike faith and just trust completely; rely on Him completely; with your entire heart, emotions, will, and thoughts. In every single thing, have complete confidence that God is able. God is able no matter what is happening right now. No matter how scary, how big, or how long it's lasted, God is able! God is able beyond your thinking, beyond your insight, beyond your understanding. This is freedom. This is *such* freedom! I'm gonna set you free from the bondage of your limited thinking and expand you to the place of the supernatural today. Expect supernatural intervention today. So jump on board with that childlike faith and let's watch God be supernatural because He's so far beyond whatever we can think or imagine.

So jump on board with childlike faith. Trust beyond your own understanding every single time. Not just once. Not just this next time. Every. Single. Time. No matter what comes. Trust beyond your own insight and understanding because it's limited. It's so limited, and God is infinite. He is all-powerful and all-knowing. He is able to do abundantly above all you can ask think or even imagine.

Ephesians 3:20 NIV says, *"Now to Him who is able to do immeasurably more than all we ask or imagine, according to His power that is at work within us."*

Chapter 12
MORE to Maybe This Time – Look Again!

I've written in this book about how the enemy comes in and says, "Maybe this time I can get them. Maybe this time they'll be too tired. They'll be too hurt. They'll be too offended. Maybe this time I can trip them up because it's just been too long or it's been too hard." The enemy comes in and he thinks, "Maybe this time?" We see that in the scripture where Jesus was tempted in the wilderness. At the end, when He rose and He was at his weakest human point (He'd been fasting. He was alone. He was in the wilderness in isolation with a lack of food. He was at his weakest point.), He overcame in victory with the Word of God. He spoke the Word and the devil had to flee. But it says (we missed that little part) at the end that the devil went just far enough off waiting for a more opportune time (Luke 4:13). That's what he does, right? He waits just far enough off for a more opportune time, thinking, *Maybe this time I'll get them.*

As I was praying and living this out (which is always what I'm coming to you with; whatever I'm living out), the Lord spoke to me that there is another side to "Maybe this time." There's another side to the enemy when he comes in with his, "Maybe this time I'll get them." There is another side to that coin. I want to show you in scripture.

Luke 5:1-11 is the passage where the disciples had been out fishing. Actually, they weren't even disciples (followers of Jesus) at this point yet. They had been out fishing all night long. These were professional fishermen. This is what they did for an occupation. They went out and they fished all night long. Listen, you may have been out doing whatever you are doing, and maybe you've been at it for a while. Maybe you've been doing all that you can to stand and you're just not seeing results at all. Maybe that's what's going on in your life right now. But I want you to read the scripture in Luke 5:8. It says that Jesus spoke to Simon, the professional fisherman that had been at it all night long. I mean some of you, you've been at this thing and you've been working so hard. You've been diligent and faithful and so here's the scripture when He had stopped speaking, He told Simon to launch out into the deep and let down his nets for a catch. "Oh come on Jesus! I already prayed for that. I've already done that. I've already been doing it. You know I mean really, why should I do this again? I should put my nets down again?" This is what the Word says: *"But Simon answered and said to Him, 'Master, we toiled all night and caught nothing.'"* (I love this! Hear this! This leaps up inside of me) *"'Nevertheless, at Your Word, I will let down the net.'"*

So let down your net again! Go ahead and let down your net again! Even if you toiled all night long. When you get the Word of the Lord inside your spirit; when you get a Word from God; when you've dug in that Word and you know what the Word of God says, at that Word, you can put down your net again! Go ahead and check again! Lower your net again! *"When they had done this they caught a great number of fish and their nets were breaking."* (Luke 5:6) They were so full. They had been at this thing for so long. They had been toiling. They had been working. And at the Word of the Lord, they were obedient to let their nets down. I like to go into every fresh day the same way: with a brand new thought on faith, and with a brand new amount of faith. I don't care what yesterday held. I don't care if I toiled and I stood and I did everything to stand. I don't care about yesterday. Today is a brand new day with brand new mercies. This is a big deal! Go ahead and let those nets down again! Don't be afraid because you didn't see the results that you wanted yesterday. At the Word of the Lord, you can go ahead and let those nets down again.

When they let their nets down again, this is what happened. Luke 5:6-10 says that this time their nets were so full of fish they began to tear! A shout for help brought their partners in the other boat, and soon both boats were filled with fish and on the verge of sinking. When Simon Peter realized what had happened, he fell to his knees before Jesus and said, "Oh, Lord, please leave me—I'm such a sinful man." For he was awestruck by the number of fish they had caught, as were the others with him. His partners, James and John, the sons of Zebedee, were also amazed. Jesus replied to Simon, "Don't be afraid! From now on you'll be fishing for people!" And as soon as they landed, they left everything and followed Jesus.

Here's another passage (this is great). 1 Kings 18 is about Elijah the prophet. There hadn't been rain for three years. This is *three years* of no rain. Elijah was a prophet that was hiding. He had been in hiding from King Ahab because the king had gone all over trying to kill him and all the prophets. God said, "Tell him it's going to rain." So Elijah had to go to King Ahab and tell him. It hadn't rained for three years, and now he had to go to this person who wanted to kill him and tell him that it was gonna rain. So he did exactly what God told him to do. He went and told the king that it was going to rain and to bring all the prophets out of Baal and they were gonna have a stand-off at Mount Carmel. So they did that. They had a stand-off. The prophets of Baal built their altar and cut the meat up and whoever sent fire was the true God. Well, of course, the prophets of Baal cut themselves and wailed and nothing happened. Elijah poured water (something that was a valuable resource because there had been a drought in the land for three years) all over his sacrifice, and the Lord sent fire and burnt up his sacrifice. So he was declaring He's the one true God. That was great evidence for Elijah, but it still hadn't rained.

He had spoken and declared that it was going to rain. So, he told the king that he should get going because it was going to rain. "I hear a mighty rainstorm coming" (1 Kings 18:41), and that was only in the spirit because there was nothing. So he climbed up to the top of the mountain, put his head between his legs and he started praying, "Oh God, send the rain," and he sent his servant to go look. He looked the first time, but there was nothing. He sent him a second time, but nothing. "Look again," he said and sent him a third time. Nothing. That may be the season that you've been in. You may have looked and looked and looked again and saw nothing coming. We've got to stand and when you've done everything to stand, stand therefore.

Because *Maybe this time.*

Maybe this time is the time you're gonna cast your net and it's gonna fill up. Maybe this time you're gonna go look and you're gonna see that cloud coming full of rain, or you're gonna see the rain coming on the horizon. Maybe this time. See, there are two sides to *Maybe this time.* The enemy's thinking *Maybe this time I can get them.* But the Lord's thinking, *Maybe this time they're gonna have faith and they're gonna look again and they're gonna see the hand of the Lord.*

So a third time, Elijah sent his servant out to look and he saw nothing. A fourth time, he sent the servant out to look. I love that kind of faith where every morning you wake up and say, "You know what? I'm gonna believe today! I didn't see it yesterday, but it doesn't matter what yesterday held. Today's a brand new day!" Let's look again! Cast our nets again. Throw them out again. So the fifth time he sent his servant out. Still nothing. The sixth time he sent his servant out...*still nothing*. Finally, for the seventh time... Come on now! *Maybe this time!* His servant saw a cloud the size of a man's fist coming in the distance and the rain had arrived!

Maybe this time! Oh, if we could get that kind of faith! If every single time, we pray with that kind of faith. But maybe this time it's gonna be the time the net is gonna be full of fish. Maybe this time is the time that I'm gonna see the cloud with rain coming on the horizon. So while the enemy's sitting over there thinking, Maybe this time I've gotten them so weakened. Maybe this time they're all alone and isolated. Maybe this time they are afraid. Maybe this time, maybe this time... We're on the other side saying, "Maybe this time is the time I'm gonna have my net overflow. Maybe this time is the time I'm gonna see that cloud coming."

You don't chop a tree down with one chop, do you? You chop, and you chop, and you chop, and you keep chopping, and if it was a big tree, you chop and chop some more. It wasn't one chop that took that tree down, and it wasn't the final chop that took that tree down. It took every single chop to take that tree down. So I'm telling you today, maybe this time! Would you go back into your situation that you just toiled over and you've given up on and think, Maybe this time. Maybe this time I'm going to come up with my nets filled with fish. Maybe this time I'm gonna see the abundance of rain. Even if you've been at this place before and toiled and you've come up empty, lukewarm, sliding into a comfort zone, and with no breakthrough. At the command of the Lord; at the Word of the Lord, cast your nets again! I'm here to tell you, cast your net again! At the Word of the Lord, cast your net again! Believe and expect that this time you're gonna come up full and overflowing and every time thereafter. On the fifth time, believe it! On the sixth time, believe it! On the seventh time, believe it! On the ninth time, just keep believing! When you've done everything that you can do stand and stand therefore, don't ever let the enemy get you with, "Maybe this time. Maybe this time it'll just feel like too much. Maybe this time it'll just feel too big. Maybe this time it'll just be too hopeless." No! Don't ever let that get you. I want you to exchange that for "Maybe this time it's gonna be the abundance of rain. Maybe this time it's gonna be our net bursting with fish."

Listen, we've got to expect and believe God every single time. No matter what we saw yesterday, no matter what battle, and no matter what giant we face. David faced Goliath and it was with little tiny stones. He just had a few little tiny stones when he faced Goliath, and he took down that giant! "Maybe this time." It's not gonna take more faith. It's not gonna take standing on your head and patting your belly, jumping on one foot. No, it's just gonna take "maybe this time." Take that stone out again. Take that little stone and put it in your sling and swing it round and round and round and watch it release and go and hit that giant and take it out!

"Maybe this time. Maybe this time." I pray that this is getting in your spirit, that this is building you up. I pray it makes you want to run out and open the door and look. Look again! I hope and I pray that it's making you want to look again. Look at your circumstance. Look at your situation again with brand new faith today. It's not that it's more faith, but at the Word of the Lord! Just get a Word from the Lord! Get in the scripture! Dig in the scripture and get a Word from the Lord and throw it out there and watch this time be different. And if it's not the next time or the next time, *maybe this time*! Don't quit! Don't give up! Don't get discouraged!

Do not let this be the time that the enemy wins; that he takes you out. That's his "maybe this time." I refuse to allow the enemy to win with "maybe this time" with me. There is no way the enemy is gonna win with "maybe this time" with me! He is such a loser! He's never won. He's always been defeated I am NOT gonna give over and resign myself to the enemy and his, Maybe this time I've got them. Maybe this time I've just got them too discouraged. Maybe this time I pushed the right button or poked the right spot."

No way! No way devil! "Maybe this time my nets are gonna be overflowing. Maybe this time I'm gonna see that cloud with the abundance of rain." This is your "maybe this time." Rise up and get excited about "maybe this time." Go look again! Cast your nets again! Swing that ax one more time because the end result is His Word goes forth and it produces what it is sent to do. When you get the Word from the Lord, it has to. It has no other choice but to produce what it is sent to do. So don't get caught up when it doesn't happen.

"But Lord we've toiled all night. We've done this. I'm a pro at this. I know what I'm doing. I've done everything exactly the way I'm supposed to do it." No – at the Word of the Lord, go cast your net again! Look again! Believe again! Believe that this time it's going to happen! At no time at all is the enemy gonna take you out. Believe maybe this time is the time that you're going to see the miracle breakthrough, and don't ever, ever give up on what you're believing for because *maybe this time.*

I hope when you hear that statement you remember both sides of it. The enemy's sitting there, "Maybe this time." I can't stand him! He's such a thief and a robber. He's such a loser. He's so defeated. He's sitting there, "Maybe this time I can just get them. Maybe this time…" Inside *our* spirit it's, "Maybe this time I'm gonna cast my net and the fish are gonna just come abundantly flowing in. Maybe this time I'm gonna look out on that horizon and I'm gonna see the cloud full of rain coming." I can't stand the thought of him just sitting there smugly thinking, *Oh I've done so well. I'm gonna trip them up.* Not now, not ever, because my "maybe this time" is I'm casting my net and I'm seeing my miracle. I pray that you, too, are gonna go into this new season casting your net again. Go look again and don't stop. Don't ever stop looking again. Don't ever lose your faith. Believe that His Word will produce. It will perform what it is sent to do. It has no other choice. Don't ever give up believing in that!